Martin H

Jesus Our Teacher

REFLECTIONS ON THE SUNDAY READINGS
FOR MATTHEW'S YEAR

the columba press

First published in 2007 by
the columba press
55A Spruce Avenue, Stillorgan Industrial Park,
Blackrock, Co Dublin

Cover by Bill Bolger
Origination by The Columba Press
Printed in Ireland by ColourBooks Ltd, Dublin

ISBN 978-1-85607-586-2

Table of Contents

Introduction

When the evangelist we call Matthew came to write his gospel, he used Mark's gospel as his primary source. He also had access to a written collection of the sayings of Jesus, and to oral traditions about Jesus. From that material he sought to write a gospel that would address the needs of his own community of believers. The resulting gospel was not simply a new edition of Mark, but a written work that has its own distinctive character.

The gospel according to Matthew is the gospel most frequently cited by church writers in the centuries following its writing. Part of its appeal was that it contained so much of Jesus' teaching. The evangelist has organised most of the teaching of Jesus into five collections: the Sermon on the Mount (5:1-7:27), mission teaching (10:5-42), parables (13:1-52), community instruction (18:1-35), and eschatological material (24:1-25:46). He concludes each of these collections in a similar fashion, viz. 'When Jesus had finished saying these things ...' (7:28; 11:1; 13:53; 19:1), with the final collection appropriately concluding, 'When Jesus had finished saying all these things ...' (26:1).

Matthew's gospel is the most Jewish of all the gospels. Jesus insists that he has been 'sent only to the lost sheep of the house of Israel' (15:24), and commands his disciples to 'go rather to the lost sheep of the house of Israel' (10:5). More than the other evangelists, Matthew makes frequent and explicit appeal to the Old Testament in telling the story of Jesus. In the first two chapters alone, he quotes from the Jewish scriptures five times. He introduces four of these quotations with the formula, 'This was to fulfil what had been spoken through the prophet ...', or a variation on that formula. There are ten occurrences of these fulfilment quotations throughout the gospel, suggesting that it was a priority for Matthew to establish that Jesus was the fulfilment of the promises contained in the Jewish scriptures.

The Jewish quality of this gospel is also evident in its concern to establish the relationship between Jesus and the Jewish Law. Matthew insists that Jesus, not the Law, is the authentic interpreter of God's will. Closely related to this is the gospel's focus on the relationship between Jesus and the Jewish guardians of the law. The conflict between Jesus and the Jewish authorities is more prominent in Matthew's gospel than in the other gospels. It is only in Matthew that Jesus says to them: 'Therefore, I tell you, the kingdom of God will be taken away from you and given to a people that produces the fruits of the kingdom' (21:43).

Although this is a very Jewish gospel, it also displays openness to the Gentiles. In the infancy narrative, Matthew's version of Jesus' genealogy includes four women, three of whom are Gentiles. While the Jewish king Herod seeks to kill the child Jesus, with the collusion of the chief priests and scribes, the Gentile Magi worship the child and place their gifts before him. In the passion narrative, while the chief priest and the elders seek to have Jesus put to death, the pagan wife of Pilate says to her husband, 'Have nothing to do with that innocent man' (27:19). As Jesus begins his Galilean ministry, Matthew cites a text from the prophet Isaiah that speaks of Galilee as 'Galilee of the Gentiles' (4:15). Commenting on Jesus' mission in Galilee, Matthew again cites a text from Isaiah that refers to the servant of God who 'will proclaim justice to the Gentiles' (12:18). The final words of Jesus direct the disciples towards the Gentiles, 'Go therefore and make disciples of all Gentiles' (28:19).

The Jewish feel of this gospel suggests that the evangelist was a Jewish Christian. The gospel is much more likely to be the work of a second generation Christian rather than that of an eyewitness. However, Matthew the eyewitness may have had some connection with the community from which the gospel emerged. A saying of Jesus that is only preserved in Matthew may contain a self-description of the evangelist. He is a 'scribe who has been trained for the kingdom of heaven', and who 'brings out of his treasure what is new and what is old' (13:52). The evangelist may have been a Jewish scribe who became a Christian and who, while proclaiming the newness of the kingdom, wishes to preserve what is best in the old.

The Jewish quality of the gospel would suggest that the community for which the gospel was written was familiar with and appreciative of Judaism. Unlike Mark, Matthew does not need to explain to his readers the traditions of the Pharisees regarding washing before meals (compare Mt 15:1-9 and Mk 7:1-13). The emphasis in the gospel on Jesus as the fulfilment of the law and the prophets suggests a community who needed reassuring that, in living the gospel, they were remaining true to their

Jewish roots. Jesus' mission is in full harmony with the will of God as expressed in the Jewish scriptures. The very negative portrayal of the Jewish leaders in the gospel may indicate that Matthew's church was in conflict with the local Jewish community or, at least, with its Pharisaic leadership, and may have been recently expelled from that community.

Yet, the gospel's openness to the Gentile mission suggests that Matthew's church, while having deep Jewish roots, was in the process of turning towards the Gentile world and, probably, had already received Gentiles into its ranks. The growing number of Gentiles entering the community may have caused tensions within it. This was a development that may have been welcomed by some, but greeted with anxiety by others. We could speak of Matthew's community as a church in transition, conscious of its Jewish roots while knowing itself to have a Gentile future. Where did Matthew's community live? Although certitude in this matter is impossible, many commentators consider Antioch, the capital of the Roman province of Syria, to be a likely candidate.

What kind of portrait of Jesus has Matthew's gospel left us? In the evangelist's account of the annunciation of Jesus' birth to Joseph, he cites from Isaiah, 'The virgin shall conceive and bear a son, and they shall name him Emmanuel, which means, "God is with us"' (1:23). At the beginning of his gospel, Matthew wants to state clearly that God is present in Jesus. Because Jesus is God-with-us, Matthew portrays people giving to Jesus the homage that is due to God alone. The Magi worship the child Jesus towards the beginning of the gospel (2:2, 8, 11), and the disciples worship the risen Lord towards the conclusion of the gospel (28:9, 17). In the course of Jesus' public ministry, the disciples worship him as Son of God (14:33).

In keeping with this more exalted portrait of Jesus in Matthew, the title 'Son of God' is a more significant title for Jesus in Matthew than in Mark. Already in the infancy narrative, with reference to the flight from Egypt, Matthew cites Hos 11:1, 'Out of Egypt I have called my son' (2:15). It is as Son of God that Jesus is tempted by Satan in the wilderness (4:3, 6) and mocked while hanging on the cross (27:40, 43). In the course of Matthew's gospel, in contrast to Mark, the disciples confess Jesus to be the Son of God (14:33; 16:16).

'Lord' is also a significant title for Jesus in this gospel. The disciples address Jesus with the title that Matthew's own church used to address the risen Jesus. This has the effect of heightening the majestic portrayal of Jesus in Matthew. In Mark's account of the storm at sea, the disciples rebuke Jesus with the question, 'Teacher, do you not care that we are perishing?' (Mk 4:38). In Matthew, the corresponding words of the disciples sound more like a prayer of Matthew's community, 'Lord, save us! We are perishing!' (8:25).

Because Jesus is God-with-us, Matthew understands him as the authoritative interpreter of God's will. In Judaism the law of God was understood as declaring God's will. However, in the Sermon on the Mount, Jesus contrasts the teaching of the law with his own teaching, 'You have heard that it was said ... but I say to you.' It is Jesus, not the Jewish law, who teaches God's will for our lives. Matthew's Jesus says of the Pharisees, who interpret God's law, 'They tie up heavy burdens, hard to bear; and lay them on the shoulders of others' (23:4). In contrast, Jesus, the authoritative interpreter of God's will, appeals to those who are burdened by the teaching of the Pharisees, 'Come to me, all you that are weary and are carrying heavy burdens, and I will give you rest. Take my yoke upon you ... For my yoke is easy, and my burden is light' (11:28-30). Because Jesus understands God's will better than the Pharisees, his teaching is not burdensome, but life giving.

In calling on people to take his yoke upon them, Jesus speaks as the Wisdom of God (cf 11:19), who invites people to submit to her yoke (cf Sir 6:19-31; 51:26). Because Jesus is the Wisdom of God, Matthew stresses that he is the only one worthy of the title 'teacher', 'You are not to be called rabbi, for you have one teacher' (23:8). The evangelist frequently presents Jesus as teaching (4:23; 5:2; 9:35; 11:1; 13:54; 21:23; 26:55), and, not surprisingly, his gospel contains a great deal of the content of that teaching. Whereas Mark states that the disciples 'taught' during Jesus' public ministry (Mk 6:30), in Matthew it is Jesus alone who teaches during this period. It is only after the death and resurrection of Jesus that the disciples start to teach. Matthew concludes his gospel with the risen and exalted Lord sharing his teaching function with his disciples (28:20).

The word 'church' occurs twice in Matthew's gospel (16:18; 18:17), although absent from the other three gospels. Matthew's own experience of church has strongly influenced his telling of the story of Jesus. In Matthew's gospel the 'now' of Jesus' ministry is also the 'now' of the church. Matthew portrays the relationship between Jesus and his disciples in ways that reflect the relationship between the risen Lord and Matthew's church. The disciples address Jesus with titles that were in frequent use within Matthew's community, such as, 'Son of God' and 'Lord'. Matthew makes a significant change to the portrayal of the disciples that he found in Mark. The latter presents the disciples in a very negative light. They do not understand; their hearts are hardened; they have no faith (cf. 8:17-21). Matthew softens this portrayal, typically presenting the disciples as people of 'little faith', standing somewhere between no faith and full faith (6:30; 8:26; 14:31; 16:8; 17:20). This portrait is shaped by Matthew's experience of his own community. Rather than people of no faith, they often display a faith that is weak, anxious and paralysed.

First Sunday of Advent

The days have been getting steadily shorter now for some time, and the shortest day of the year is still over three weeks away. Yet, today, the beginning of the church's year, the first Sunday of Advent, a light begins to shine in the darkness, symbolised by the lighting of the first candle of the Advent wreath. The call at the end of today's first reading expresses the change of mood: 'Let us walk in the light of the Lord.' Advent brings light to the dark days of winter. It is a time when we wait in joyful hope for the coming of our Saviour Jesus Christ. It is good to allow some of the joyful anticipation of Advent to rub off on us a little, to allow ourselves to be touched by this waiting in joyful hope.

We often find it difficult to wait. Waiting does not come easy to us. The commercial world cannot wait for Christmas. The carols of Christmas have been piping through our department stores for some weeks now. Our shop windows are already full of the tinsel and glitter of Christmas. In one way, there is little to be done about all of this. Yet, we can, to some extent, step back from it all and consciously enter into the spirit of joyful waiting that Advent invites us to. That spirit is well captured in our response to today's psalm: I rejoiced when I heard them say 'Let us go to God's house.' These words were spoken by pilgrims as they set out on pilgrimage to the temple in Jerusalem. They anticipated with great joy the prospect of arriving at the beautiful temple. This was the joy of expectation. It is the joy of Advent. We joyfully look forward to celebrating the birth of our Saviour and all that his birth has come to mean for us.

We all need something to look forward to. The first reading of the first Sunday of Advent invites us to look forward to a better world where justice and peace are more plentiful than they presently are. God knows, it can be an effort at times to conjure up the prospect of a more just and peaceful world. Yet we cannot allow ourselves to loose the capacity to imagine something better. Isaiah's vision of swords being hammered into ploughshares and of sickles being hammered into spears was one of the inspirational texts for the founding of the United Nations after the Second World War. Isaiah's inspirational vision moved people to action in ways he could not have anticipated. We can never underestimate the power of imagination to shape things for the better. Advent invites us to dream God's dream for our world; it calls on us to be faithful to that dream, to live out of it, so that it becomes more of a reality among us than it presently is.

Advent stirs in us the desire to reach forward to grasp a better future, the future that God is always holding out to us. Those who were once bitter enemies are called to find ways of hammering weapons of war into instruments of peace. Advent prompts all of us to leave behind old patterns of thinking, behaving and relating and to grasp something new. This first Sunday of Advent calls on us to look forward rather than to look back, in the words of Paul's letter to the Philippians, 'straining forward to what lies ahead'.

Both the second reading and the gospel reading today issue a wake up call. 'Wake up now', says Paul. 'Stay awake', says Jesus. When we wake up and get out of bed in the morning, we turn our faces towards the day that lies ahead, sometimes with a bit of a struggle. Getting out of bed expresses our willingness to face the day. Advent invites us to wake up and to turn our faces towards the day of the Lord. It calls on us to be awake to what the Lord wants, to live each day as the Lord wants it to be lived. In this way the future that the Lord desires will become more of a reality among us.

Being alert to what the Lord wants will often mean leaving behind ways and patterns that are not part of God's future. Paul mentions drunken orgies, promiscuity, wrangling and jealousy. We can all make up our own list, probably a much less spectacular one than Paul's. Advert calls on us to be alert to everything within us and among us that can have no place in God's future. Such alertness fires our resolve to reach out and grasp what the Lord is offering us. The awareness of our own weaknesses disposes us to welcome the Lord whose coming to us as Saviour is assured.

Second Sunday of Advent

Now that the second Sunday of Advent is upon us, the count-down to Christmas has begun in earnest. The Christmas decorations are going up in our homes. Images of Santa Claus are beginning to abound. The gospel reading for this Sunday presents us with someone who is as far removed from the average cuddly Santa as you can get. John the Baptist is unlikely to find himself on any Christmas tree. This man of the wilderness, whose dress sense and diet are decidedly unfashionable, seems out of place in the Christmas rush. His way of addressing respectable people as 'Brood of vipers!' strikes a rather jarring note in this season of goodwill towards all. Just as the songs of Christmas declare that it is the season to be jolly, John bellows 'Repent.' The smiling baby with hands raised in our cribs is a far cry from the 'more powerful' one that John talks about, who arrives with a winnowing-fan in his hand, ready to separate wheat from chaff.

What are we to do with this strange prophet who seems so out of season? The temptation is to ignore him, on the grounds that we have enough to cope with in the run up to Christmas. Many of his contemporaries did ignore him. Herod, the political ruler of Galilee, went further; he had John beheaded. Yet, in today's gospel reading we are told that 'Jerusalem and all Judea and the whole Jordan district made their way to him.' Large crowds travelled out into the wilderness and submitted to John's baptism, confessing their sins. His challenging message, his call to repent, seems to have struck some deep chord in them. If he can strike a chord in his contemporaries, he may even be able to strike a chord in us. Perhaps, after all, we can make room for John and his message in the Christmas rush.

John the Baptist may not be a Christmas figure, but he certainly is an Advent saint. He belongs to the season of Advent, just as surely as Jesus, Mary and Joseph belong to the feast of Christmas. If we are to take Advent seriously, we have to take John the Baptist seriously too, and if we are not serious about the season of Advent, we cannot claim to be serious about the feast of Christmas. John saw clearly that someone much more important than himself was coming, and that people needed to get ready for his appearance. He continues to call on us today to prepare a way in our lives for the Lord. John takes the emphasis away from preparing for Christmas and puts it on preparing for Christ. In Advent John puts it up to us to do whatever is necessary to receive Christ more fully into our lives at Christmas. His call to repent is a call to turn away from whatever in our lives is blocking Christ from coming to live in us and through us.

Today's gospel reading suggests that John was intolerant of complacency. His harshest words were for those religious leaders who repeatedly declared, 'We have Abraham for our father', and who were so content in that knowledge that they never looked seriously at their own lives. We know from experience that we are all prone to complacency. The awareness that we have done nothing seriously wrong can leave us content. We can drift along feeling reasonably pleased with ourselves most of the time. We can be intolerant of those who might suggest otherwise. John's voice continues to call out to us to look seriously at our lives and to ask ourselves what needs to change if our lives are to bear good fruit, the fruit of Christ. John reminds us that we are not yet all that the Lord is calling us to be. He refuses to leave us where we are and, instead, he asks us to keep setting out on a journey.

John's message on its own could leave us feeling a bit discouraged. In finding ourselves knocked off our complacent perches, we might struggle to get up again. In a sense, John's baptism of water can only bring us so far. We need the one whom John announced, the one who baptises with the Holy Spirit, if we are to move further. We cannot become all that the Lord is calling us to be without the help of that Holy Spirit. We need the Spirit of the Lord that Isaiah the prophet speaks about in the first reading. Advent is a season when we invite the Spirit afresh into our lives, so that Christ may be formed in us, as he was in Mary. It is only in the power of the Spirit that our lives can bear the good fruit that John the Baptist calls for.

Third Sunday of Advent

We normally think of John the Baptist as a strong man of the wilderness – physically strong and unyielding in his convictions. That is the portrait of John we are given in the gospels. Yet, today's gospel reading reveals a more vulnerable side to John the Baptist. There he is in Herod's dark prison, wracked with doubt, wondering if the person he had identified as the Messiah – Jesus of Nazareth – was really the Messiah after all. From his prison cell he sends one of his followers to ask Jesus, 'Are you the one who is to come, or have we to wait for someone else?' John was really asking himself, 'Have I got it wrong?'

Jesus had not quite turned out as John had expected. John had announced that Jesus would be rather like himself, a fiery prophet, with his winnowing fan in his hand, gathering the wheat into his barn and burning the chaff in unquenchable fire. However, Jesus was not quite the fiery prophet that John had announced. He was much more the messenger of God's mercy than of God's judgement.

It is often the way in life that what happens is not what we expect to happen. People who are significant for us can take paths that surprise and even disappoint us. Plans that we might have cherished do not materialise as we would have liked. Hopes we had entertained for some situation or other come to nothing. At such times we can easily identify with John the Baptist's puzzled question at the beginning of today's gospel reading. The loss of some precious hope or expectation or plan can unsettle us and leave us asking questions of ourselves and of the Lord. We can loose heart and get discouraged. The fight and the fire can go out of us. Our faith can be undermined.

As part of his response to John's puzzled question, Jesus pronounced a beatitude, 'Happy is the one who does not lose faith in me.' Jesus was calling on John not to lose faith, not to lose heart, in the midst of his confusion and disappointment. In our own dark times when we struggle to let go of some of our most cherished hopes and dreams, the Lord makes the same call on us not to lose faith in him. This is also the message of today's first reading, 'Strengthen all weary hands, steady all trembling knees, and say to all faint hearts, "Courage! Do not be afraid".

Look your God is coming.' No matter how bitter disappointment, how great our loss, it is always the case that the Lord is coming. This is the great message of Advent. In the words of today's responsorial psalm, 'It is the Lord who keeps faith forever'. Because the Lord keeps faith forever, because he is always faithful to us, we need not lose faith in him, even when so much else fails us.

That first reading from Isaiah speaks of a wilderness and a wasteland. John the Baptist was in his own wasteland and wilderness as he struggled with great doubt in Herod's cell. Each of us can find ourselves in something of a wilderness for a whole variety of reasons. Indeed, for many people these days coming up to Christmas and the days over Christmas can be something of a wilderness time. Such people find it very hard to enter into spirit of Christmas celebration. The readings of this third Sunday of Advent assure us that we are not alone in the wilderness. The God in whom we believe is one who comes into our various wildernesses to transform them into places of new life. God comes to us through his Son who makes the deaf hear, the blind see, the lame walk, who restores the dead to life and proclaims good news to the poor.

The Lord comes to us where we are, as we are, in our need, in our struggles, with our doubts and disappointments. He does not ask us to leave where we are and to meet him in some rarefied space. He speaks into, comes into, our own personal wilderness, just as he spoke into John's prison cell. That is what we celebrate at Christmas. The Word became flesh and dwelt among us. Through his Son, God comes into our lives in all their frailty and vulnerability. We do not have to step out of where we are to look for him. He is there already with us in the midst of it, 'waiting at the gates', in the words of today's second reading. We pray that in these days coming up to the feast of Christmas we would experience the Lord's coming to us and that his coming would keep us hopeful in the midst of our disappointments and losses.

Fourth Sunday of Advent

This Sunday the fourth candle on our Advent wreath has been lit. The only candle remaining to be lit now is the white one which will be lit on Christmas day. The short season of Advent is drawing to a close; the feast of Christmas is almost upon us. This is reflected in the readings for this Sunday. The Advent figure of John the Baptist, who has featured in the gospel reading for the last two Sundays, now gives way to the figures that we associate with the feast of Christmas, Mary, Joseph, and their child, Jesus. We are on the brink of entering into the Christmas story.

When reading the gospels, I have always found it helpful to focus on the various characters that appear in the gospel story. They are men and women with the same hopes and struggles that we all have. We can recognise something of ourselves in all of them. The person who features most prominently in today's gospel reading is Joseph. It is strange how Christian art has tended to portray Joseph as an old man, more like Jesus' grandfather or great-grandfather, than Jesus' father. One striking exception to this is the painting of Joseph by the Spanish artist, El Greco. He depicts Joseph as a vigorous young man, with Jesus clinging to his legs. In that painting Joseph is portrayed as a strong figure, trustworthy and protective. This is much closer to the portrayal of Joseph in the gospels than the usual elderly depiction of him.

In today's gospel reading Joseph is referred to as a man of honour. In other words, he was a decent man. In the complex situations of life, he tried to do the right thing, what he believed God wanted of him. Mary's unexplained pregnancy left this young man in a very difficult situation. Presuming that her pregnancy indicated she had been unfaithful to him, Joseph found himself torn between what he understood God's law required him to do, to divorce Mary, and his own affectionate feelings for her. In this confusing situation, the gospel reading tells us that Joseph received guidance from the Lord – guidance he promptly followed.

The complex situation in which Joseph found himself is not unlike the kind of situations in which many of us find ourselves from time to time. In so many of life's situations the best way forward is not always immediately clear. Like Joseph in the gospel reading, we can find ourselves torn between what our head is telling us and what our heart is saying to us. The course of action we might initially decide to take does not always turn out to be the right option, just as the path that Joseph originally intended to take was not the one that the Lord was asking him to take. The temptation can be to rush into taking the path that first occurs to us. The better thing can often be to take time, to step back and to ask the Lord to enlighten us and to guide us.

We can sometimes find it difficult to acknowledge to ourselves and to others that we are unclear about what is best to do. We can place too much reliance on our own judgement. The gospel reading today invites us to have something of the openness of Joseph to the Lord's guidance. That guidance is given to those who ask for it. Joseph received the Lord's guidance through an angel. The Lord's guidance will come to us through more ordinary means, such as through those in whom we confide. It is often the way that clarity is found by sharing our confusion, our distress, with one or two trusted others. Their perspective on the situation we are struggling with can often bring a new and a fresh light, one we could not have hit upon if left to ourselves. We can also experience the Lord's guidance through prayer. In prayer we allow the Lord to enlighten our minds and hearts so that we can move forward in the light that he provides.

According to the gospel reading, the child that was born of Mary was called Emmanuel, God-with-us. Through Jesus, God is present to all of us in a strikingly new way. The Lord has chosen to be with us as our companion on the way, to guide us in moments of confusion and struggle, to sustain us in moments of weakness, to heal us in moments of brokenness, to assure us of God's forgiveness in times of failure. We prepare for the feast of Christmas by acknowledging our own need of Jesus, Emmanuel. This Sunday we are invited to approach the coming feast with something of the same openness to the Lord's presence and guidance that Joseph showed in today's gospel reading.

Christmas: Midnight Mass

Children have a wonderful way of entering into the story of the first Christmas. It is a story that they identify with quite easily. The nativity play captures their imagination; they play their parts with enthusiasm, whether it is the part of the shepherds or the angels, or the wise men, or Mary and Joseph. It is a story that is very accessible to them. At Christmas we celebrate the good news that God has become accessible, not just to children, but to all of us. God is now revealed in a human life, in a life that began as all our lives began, as a vulnerable and helpless infant. New born children are very accessible, very engaging; they draw us towards themselves. We find ourselves getting close to them. We love to take them up in our arms and to hold them for a while. They have nothing to say to us and, yet, they communicate with us very powerfully, so powerfully that we can become oblivious to others as long as we have them in our arms.

In and through Mary and Joseph's new born child, God was communicating with us very powerfully. Matthew in his gospel names this child Emmanuel, God-with-us. There is a sense in which every new born child is Emmanuel, God-with-us. Every new born child is an image of God and reveals God the Creator. As Christians we believe that the new born child of Mary and Joseph was Emmanuel in a unique sense. That is why as Christians we have been celebrating his birth every year for the last two thousand years. We celebrate this child's birth every year because we know who this child became. It is because the adult Jesus has in some way spoken to us and engaged us that we celebrate his birth. It is because we know that he lived and died and rose from the dead for us that his birth is so important to us. It is because we believe that this child of Mary and Joseph is, in the words of today's gospel reading, Saviour, Christ and Lord that we recognise his birth as good news to be celebrated.

As we return to our homes after this Mass, it is worth remembering why we are celebrating. We celebrate because, in the words of the angels to the shepherds in the gospel reading, we have heard 'news of great joy, a joy to be shared by the whole people'. The good news is that God has drawn near to us in and through a human life. In doing so God has shown us what God is really like, and God has also shown us what being truly human is really like. Jesus, who was both fully divine and fully human, reveals God to us and also reveals ourselves to us.

We receive this revelation primarily from the adult Jesus rather than the child Jesus. Even though at Christmas we celebrate the birth of the child Jesus, it is really a feast, like all the Christian feasts, that calls on us to focus on the adult Jesus who lived, died and rose from the dead and who, as risen Lord, is as present to us today as the child Jesus was present to Mary and Joseph. He is present to us this Christmas night as we gather to celebrate the Eucharist. In coming to the Eucharist tonight we are like the shepherds in the gospel reading who hurried away from their flocks to Bethlehem to welcome and receive this gift of God that had been made known to them. The gospel reading says that having gone to Bethlehem and found what had been told to them, they went back to their flocks glorifying and praising God for all they had heard and seen. They went back to share what they had received, as we too are called to do.

The shepherds went to Bethlehem to receive the child Jesus. We come to the Eucharist to receive the risen Lord. In receiving him in the Eucharist we are at the same time invited to receive him more fully into our lives, so that he can continue to live his life in and through our lives. That is the great Christmas calling, the great Christian calling. The Lord wants to be born anew within each one of us. He wants to live and work in us and through us. When we allow him to do so, our lives become good news for others. As an adolescent, Jesus said to his parents, 'I must be about my Father's business.' The risen Lord continues to be about God's business in and through all our lives. This Christmas night we open our lives anew to the Lord and to all he wants to do through us.

Christmas: Day Mass

At the centre of the Christmas story is a family – a mother, a father and their new born child. The word 'God' can suggest someone remote, very far above us, somewhat inaccessible. However, there is nothing more accessible than a new born baby. Everyone wants to get close to a new born baby. They exert a certain fascination on all of us. We look at this new bundle of life, mesmerised. The parents who are here this morning know that better than I do. Christmas celebrates the extraordinary good news that the new born child of Mary and Joseph is God-with-us, Emmanuel. Those who looked into the eyes of this child were looking into the eyes of God. It is hard to imagine how God could have become more accessible to us than by taking the form of a new born child. If God wanted to draw close to us, to engage us, to draw us into relationship, this was a very good way to do it. In Jesus, the first born child of Mary and Joseph, God became vulnerable, accessible, engaging.

Perhaps that is why the feast of Christmas continues to engage us at the more spiritual level of our make up. Yes, Christmas has become overly commercialised. We all spend more than we need to; if we are not careful we can easily go overboard and get ourselves into unnecessary debt. Yet, the numbers who come to church on Christmas day are always well up on other times of the year. God, who reached out to us through a new born babe, continues to draw us at this time of the year. It somehow feels right to come to church on this day of all days. It is as if we sense, at some level, that if God has gone to such lengths to connect with us, the least we can do is attempt to connect with God. Like the shepherds in Luke's account of the birth of Jesus, we hear the call to come to the crib. On reaching it, we are invited to let our eyes and our minds roam free as we ponder the wonderful mystery of Jesus' birth, the mystery of Emmanuel, God-with-us.

Mary and Joseph's child, of course, became an adult, a vigorous young man who placed his life's energy at the disposal of God the Father for the service of all men and woman. As an adult Jesus declared of himself, 'The Son of Man came not to be served but to serve and to give his life as a ransom for many.' He gave his life for us all and, having been raised from the dead, he continues to give himself to us all. Indeed, at this Eucharist which we now celebrate, the risen Lord gives himself to each of us as the bread of life. We come here on this Christmas morning not only to ponder the image of the child Jesus in the crib, but to receive into our lives the glorious and risen adult Jesus in the Eucharist. He calls us who are adults into an adult relationship with him. He says to us what he said to his disciples on the night before he died, 'I no longer call your servants, I call you friends.' He waits for us to reciprocate, to befriend him as he has befriended us, to reach out towards him as he has reached out towards us, to accept him as our companion on our life's way.

The second reading this morning speaks of God's Son as 'the radiant light of God's glory'. When John the evangelist wanted to express the mystery of this feast of Christmas, he wrote: 'A light … shines in the darkness, a light that darkness could not overpower.' The adult Jesus spoke of himself as the light of the world and promised that those who follow him will never walk in darkness. Many of us today experience a sense of darkness in one form of another. It might be the darkness of depression, of illness, of a broken relationship, of a deep loss, or the darkness that envelopes us when we look at all that is not right with our world. At Christmas we celebrate the coming of Jesus as light into our darkness. On this Christmas morning, we might make our own a wonderful prayer of John Henry Newman, a great scholar and writer of the nineteenth century, an Anglican who became a Roman Catholic. It is a prayer addressed to the risen Jesus as light in our darkness: 'Lead kindly light amid the encircling gloom, lead Thou me on. The night is dark and I am far from home, lead Thou me on. I do not ask to see the distant scene. One step enough for me.'

Feast of the Holy Family

Christmas is very much a family time. Most of us will have made contact with our families over the Christmas. If we cannot meet up in person, we will phone or email or write. We instinctively feel that Christmas is a time to make more of an effort than we might normally make to connect with each other within the family.

Today we celebrate the feast of one particular family, the family of Jesus. We traditionally speak of this family as the holy family, and we usually think of it as a family of three, Jesus, Mary and Joseph. Yet, these three would have thought of their family in a much wider sense. The extended family was very important in Jesus' time and culture, as it is today in many parts of the world.

Many of us will have happy memories of our extended family. When I was a child, I was fortunate to have had two wonderful aunts who never married. Every Thursday they would come to our house with gifts for the children, and they would stay with us for a few hours while my parents went to the pictures. It was a night out for my parents and a treat for myself and my brothers. I am sure many people here this morning would acknowledge the hugely significant influence of members of the extended family on their own upbringing, whether it was the influence of grandparents, aunts, uncles, cousins. I wonder have we lost something of that value of the extended family today. Has the nuclear family retreated into a narrower, more private space? If so, we are losing something important.

In any close-knit group, tensions are inevitable, and the family group is no different. St. Paul's words in today's second reading addressed to the family of the church are pertinent for all family life. He calls on us to be clothed with sincere compassion, kindness, humility, gentleness, patience, and then over all those clothes to put on the garment of love. This is the baptismal wardrobe. It is the wardrobe we need if tensions are not to develop into rifts. This wardrobe is not one we make for ourselves. It is given to us by the Lord; it is the fruit of his Spirit in our lives. We need to pray for this wardrobe, to call on that Spirit to bear his rich fruit in our lives. To the extent that we put on these clothes, the peace of Christ will reign in our hearts and in our homes.

Not only are tensions inevitable in families, so also is suffering and pain. For many families Christmas can be a very painful time. The pain of separation from family members who have died can be felt more keenly at Christmas than at other times of the year. That separation can be due to death or to other reasons such as estrangement or physical distance. The general mood of celebration at Christmas time can make the pain within some families all the more pronounced. Today's gospel reading reminds us that the holy family was no stranger to pain, suffering and loss. According to Matthew, this family was separated from their relatives and their home shortly after Jesus was born. They became refugees in a foreign land, wanting to return home but unable to do so because of the oppressive ruler in their land. The picture that is painted by today's gospel reading is the reality for many of the refugee families in our midst this Christmas. Our attitude to such families makes a statement about our attitude to the holy family.

The suffering of families who are native to this land will take different forms. Some families will have members who are seriously ill at this time, perhaps in hospital. The energies of family members will be going into supporting the sick family member. The exhortation at the end of today's first reading is striking: 'Support your father in his old age … do not despise him in your health and strength.' In our health and strength we are called to support the weak and the frail, in the knowledge that the day will come when our own health and strength will fail. Many a family is engaged in that work at this Christmas time. It is the Lord's work, and they can be assured of the Lord's help in the doing of it.

As we look ahead towards a new year, we might ask ourselves if there are members of our family we need to connect with more fully. Today's gospel reading describes a journey of the holy family away from home and then back towards home again. There may be journeys we need to make in order to find anew some family member who has drifted from us.

Solemnity of Mary, Mother of God

Because we have grown so accustomed to our yearly celebration of the feast of Christmas, it can happen that the events we celebrate at Christmas no longer surprise us. We can easily cease to be amazed at them. Today on the feast of Mary, Mother of God, which is the octave day of Christmas, we see Mary, in the gospel reading, marvelling at what has happened, treasuring the events of Christmas in her memory, and pondering them in her heart.

The image of Mary put before us in this morning's gospel reading is that of the contemplative woman who ponders the marvels the Almighty has done for her and for all people. She ponders in response to what the shepherds said to her. The shepherds had preached the gospel to her. They repeated to her what had been told to them by the angels, 'Today in the town of David, a Saviour has been born to you; he is Christ the Lord.' This is the good new of great joy, the gospel. These lowly shepherds are the first to hear the gospel and the first preachers of the gospel, according to Luke. Mary was the first to hear the gospel from the shepherds. It is this gospel that she treasured and pondered over. The same gospel has been preached to us, and we are invited to treasure that gospel, to ponder on it and to respond to it, as Mary did.

Today is new year's day, a day to make resolutions. What better new year's resolution could we make today than that of adopting Mary's stance before the gospel of the Word made flesh, making her contemplative gaze our own, keeping the incarnate God constantly before our mind and heart. Today's feast invites us to share in Mary's sense of awe and wonder before God's merciful love, made known to us in Christ, Mary's son. As we look back over the past year, we can ask ourselves how much of it has been spent in the imitation of Mary, the silent one, who pondered God's sayings and doings in her heart. As we look towards the new year, which begins today, we ask Mary to help us to treasure the gospel as she did, so that we might bring forth Christ in our lives as Mary brought forth Christ as his mother.

As mother of Jesus, Mary was hugely influential in his shaping and formation. Jesus must have received and learned a great deal from her, as all of us have received and learned much from our mothers. She nurtured him; she taught him the religious traditions of her people; she guided him through childhood and adolescence. Although Mary went on to become the foremost disciple of Jesus, there is a sense in which it can be said that Jesus lived the earlier years of his life as her disciple. Mary, the mother of Jesus, the mother of God, is also the mother of the church, as declared by the Second Vatican Council. She is mother of all of Jesus' disciples. As disciples of her Son, we have a great deal to learn from her, just as Jesus learned much from her in his early years. We look to her to show us what it means to be a disciple of her Son.

Living as we are in an age when we can take so much for granted, including the treasure of the gospel we have received, it is perhaps Mary's deeply appreciative and reflective stance towards the gospel that has most to teach us today. The Spirit that came upon Mary at the annunciation, that came upon Jesus at his baptism and that came upon the church at Pentecost, has come upon all of us at baptism. In pondering the gospel as Mary did, we will be allowing the Spirit whom God has sent into our hearts to shape and mould us more completely. This is the Spirit that cries out from deep within us, 'Abba, Father', as Paul reminds us in today's second reading. Because of her treasuring and pondering God's word, Mary was a woman of the Spirit. Her life was led by the Spirit. That is our calling too.

Second Sunday after Christmas

We have just begun a new year. There is something hopeful about the beginning of a new year. It is a time of new beginning. We let go of the old year and head out into something new. Nature is also on the verge of a new beginning. Even though we are in mid winter, we know that each day is now that little bit longer than the previous one. With the lengthening of the daylight, there comes an emergence of new life. Although nature looks quite dead at the moment, we are aware that new life is beginning to stir. Soon the first snowdrops and crocuses will begin to put their heads above the earth.

Today's gospel reading reflects this moment of new beginning with its growing light. The gospel reading speaks of a light that shines in the darkness, a light that darkness cannot overpower, a true light that enlightens everyone. The gospel reading is referring, of course, not to the light of the sun, but to a different quality of light. It is the light of the Word who was with God in the beginning. Because this Word became flesh, his light has become accessible to us. It is not a distant light, like a distant star, that can only be seen with a strong telescope. It is a light that envelopes all our living. The gospel reading is reminding us that we live and move in this special light. Later on in John's gospel, Jesus says of himself: 'I am the light of the world. Whoever follows me will never walk in darkness but will have the light of life.'

'A light shines in the darkness, a light that darkness could not overpower.' I have always found that statement in today's gospel reading to be one of the most hopeful statements in all of the New Testament. We have all known our own dark times. A darkness of spirit can engulf us; we can find ourselves getting depressed for some reason or other. A darkness of mind can also come over us; we find it hard to think clearly; we struggle to find a clear way forward out of some complex situation. We can find ourselves dealing with a darkness of heart, assailed by dark feelings that leave us feeling guilty and ashamed. Or we can be suddenly plunged into some dark and difficult situation that we had not anticipated. It might be an experience of bereavement or some other form of loss, a sudden onset of illness, in our own lives or in the life of a loved one, some major disappointment or an experience of personal failure. The dark experience, whatever form it takes, can threaten to overwhelm us. We might even find it hard to get out of bed in the morning and to face the day. The future seems uninviting.

It is to those kinds of situations that today's gospel reading can speak most powerfully. The evangelist declares that there is no human darkness which the light of Christ cannot and does not penetrate. There is no human affliction that cannot be endured with the Lord's help. There is a lot of talk today about resource people. Today's gospel reading assures us that the Lord is a resource to us all whenever we struggle with some dark experience. He is the true light that enlightens everyone. The Word became flesh and dwelt among us full of grace and truth, so that we might all receive from his fullness. The life-giving light of Christ shines on all our lives.

The gospel reading acknowledges that people can turn away from this light. The true light was in the world and the world did not know him. A little later in John's gospel the evangelist says: 'The light has come into the world, and people loved darkness rather than light.' There remains the mystery of human freedom, the freedom to turn away from what is good, wholesome and life-giving. The Lord recognises that freedom. At one point in the gospel of John, he turns to his closest disciples and says to them: 'Do you also wish to go away?' Yet, that light of God that Jesus embodies continues to shine upon us and to invite us, even when we turn away from it. The presence of that light in our lives is not dependent on how well we receive it, just as the light of the sun does not grow weak when we try to shut it out. The Lord never turns away from us, and the light of his love never ceases to shine upon us. This is the good news we celebrate in the season of Christmas. It is what makes Christmas special.

The Feast of the Epiphany

We know from our experience that different people can respond in different ways to the same event. Today's gospel reading puts before us two very contrasting responses to the news that the long-awaited Jewish Messiah had just been born. Astrologers from the East were so excited by this news that they set out on a long journey to find the child so as to pay him homage. King Herod in Jerusalem was so perturbed by the same news that he sought to kill the child.

Today on this feast of the Epiphany we are asked to identify with the response of the astrologers, the wise men, from the East. They were people who were very observant of nature, God's natural world, in particular that dimension of God's natural world that came into view when darkness descended. They observed and studied the stars. Yet, they were not so fascinated by the stars that they worshipped the stars. They recognised that the stars, for all their splendour, pointed beyond themselves to some more wonderful reality, to God. So, when they heard that God was visiting our world in a new way through a Jewish child who had just been born, they set out in search of that child. These exotic figures from the East show us how being attentive to God's natural world can draw us closer to God. This can happen in different ways for different people. For the wise men it was their fascination with the stars that led them to the true light of the world. The redness of a rose spoke to Joseph Mary Plunket of the redeeming death of Christ. God can speak to us in a variety of ways through the world of nature. The wise men teach us to be attentive and observant of that world, so that in and through it we may experience the presence of the living God.

There came a point on the journey of the wise men when they needed more than the signs of nature to find the child whom they were seeking. To make the last short step on their long journey, they needed more than the light of a star. They needed the light of the scriptures. The chief priests and the scribes who knew the scriptures were able to point them in the direction of Bethlehem. On our own journey towards the Lord, we too need the light of the scriptures as well as the light of nature. The scriptures are a fuller revelation of God than the natural world. It is in and through the scriptures that we meet God and his Son in a special way. St Jerome, one of the great saints of the church and a scripture scholar of his time, said that ignorance of the scriptures is ignorance of Christ. Through the scriptures God speaks to us in a privileged way. He asks us to listen and to allow our lives to be shaped by what we hear. The wise men allowed themselves to be guided by the scriptures, as well as by the star. They showed something of that responsiveness to God's word to which we are all called.

Having been moved by the presence of God in nature and in the scriptures, the wise men came face to face with God in a child. They did not worship the star; they did not even worship the scriptures. But they did worship the child, because they recognised that here was Emmanuel, God-with-us. We too worship Emmanuel, and we do so in a special way every time we celebrate the Eucharist, as we are doing today. As the wise men expressed their worship by offering the child their precious gifts, we express our own worship of the Lord in the Eucharist by offering him our lives. We give ourselves to him in response to his giving of himself to us as bread of life. As the Lord says to us: 'Take, this is my body', we place ourselves before the Lord, saying: 'Here I am, I come to do your will.'

The gospel reading tells us that, after worshipping the child, the wise men returned home by a different way. Their meeting with the infant king of the Jews somehow changed them. Our own worship of the Lord in the Eucharist will prompt us to take a different path too. We come to the Eucharist open to being changed by the Lord who comes to us. As we receive the body of Christ, we seek to become more fully the body of Christ in the world. We are sent forth from the Eucharist to follow the way of the Lord more closely. We pray on this feast of the Epiphany that we would be as open to the Lord's presence and call as the wise men in today's gospel reading.

The Baptism of the Lord

It is impossible for us not to have favourites. We invariably favour some people over others. It is because we favour some and not others that we include some people among our friends and not others. Even among our friends we favour some over others. Marriage between two people occurs because one man favours one woman out of other women and that woman favours that man out of other men. There are contexts, however, in which showing favour is not appropriate. Politicians have got themselves into trouble because they used their influence inappropriately to favour someone. The human tendency to show favour, while natural, sometimes needs to be kept in check.

In today's second reading, Peter, addressing Cornelius and his household, says: 'The truth I have come to realise is that God does not have favourites.' It sounds as if Peter has only recently hit upon this truth. As a Jew, he would have understood that God did have favourites. The Jewish people were the chosen people who had been graced by God in a unique way. However, since his meeting with Jesus, Peter had come to realise that God does not have favourites. If God had favoured the people of Israel in the past, it was for the sake of all the other nations. God chose Israel not because God loved Israel more than all the other nations, but because God wanted Israel to be the messenger of God's love to all the nations. According to today's first reading, God chose Israel as his servant, to be the light of the nations.

Jesus came as the servant of all people, to give his life as a ransom for all. At the very end of his gospel, Matthew portrays the risen Jesus telling his disciples to go and make disciples of all the nations. All nations are to be favoured with the gospel. That is why we find Peter in today's second reading preaching to the pagan centurion Cornelius and his household, and then going on to baptise them all. Our own baptism is the direct result of that command of the risen Jesus to baptise all nations. Baptism is a sign of God's favour. On the day of our baptism God said to us what was said to Jesus on the day of his baptism: 'My favour rests on you.' God also acted to show his favour to us by pouring the Holy Spirit into our hearts at baptism. Parents instinctively understand baptism as an expression of God's favour. That is why they bring their children to be baptised. Today on the feast of Jesus' baptism, we give thanks for our own baptism, this very special sign of God's favour.

The baptism of Jesus was not only the day when he had a special experience of God's favour; it was also the day when he publicly took on the role of God's servant. Jesus' baptism was both a grace and a commission. As Peter announced to Cornelius in today's second reading, after his baptism Jesus went about doing good and curing all who had fallen into the power of the devil. Today's first reading, although written long before Jesus was born, describes this mission of Jesus very well. He brings true justice to the nations; by his words and deeds, Jesus makes known the just or right way that God wants us all to take and that Jesus took to the full. In making known God's justice, that first reading also declares that he 'does not break the crushed reed, nor quench the wavering flame'. Jesus' mission was characterised by a heightened awareness of the weak and the vulnerable.

Our own baptism, like that of Jesus, was both a gift and a commission. In bestowing favour upon us, God at the same time calls us to become his servants. On the day of our baptism, we are commissioned as servants of God, after the example of Jesus. As God endowed Jesus with the Spirit so that he could bring true justice to the nations, at our baptism we were endowed with the same Spirit for the same purpose. In the power of the Spirit we are called to live in that same just way that Jesus lived. In the words of the first reading, baptism calls us to 'serve the cause of right'. That will involve for us, as it did for Jesus, taking care not 'to break the crushed reed, nor quench the wavering flame'. Those who are crushed for whatever reason, whose flame is barely flickering, are deserving of our greatest care and attention. We show that we really appreciate the gift of our baptism when we support the vulnerable and strengthen the weak, in our families, our communities and our society. This is our baptismal calling.

First Sunday of Lent

It has often been said that conflict in life is inevitable. What matters is how such conflict is dealt with. We can find ourselves from time to time in some form of conflict with others. We sometimes need to call on a third party to help us to resolve such conflict. We can also be aware of conflict within ourselves; we can be pulled in two different directions at once. Sometimes we know deep down that one of the two directions we are being pulled in will not serve us or others well. We have traditionally spoken of this as an experience of temptation.

The gospel reading describes Jesus' experience of temptation. We are given a glimpse into an inner conflict as he begins his public ministry. At his baptism, Jesus had an experience of God his Father, assuring him that he was the beloved Son, and filling him with the Holy Spirit. Shortly after his baptism in the Jordan, he had a very different kind of experience in the wilderness, an experience of Satan, tempting him to take a very different path to the one on which his baptism had launched him. At his baptism, Jesus was sent forth by the Father in the service of others; in the wilderness, Satan tempts him to be self-serving – to look out for his own physical needs, to gain a following by indulging in the spectacular, to sell his soul for the sake of power and status. The gospel reading portrays what must have been a very real conflict within Jesus. At the very end of Jesus' public ministry, we are given a glimpse of another conflict within him. In the Garden of Gethsemane, he struggled with the temptation to avoid the cross that lay before him by pulling back from the mission which began at his baptism. On both occasions, at the beginning and end of his ministry, in the wilderness and in Gethsemane, Jesus resisted the temptation that assailed him. He resolved his inner conflict in favour of remaining faithful to God's call and to the mission that God had entrusted to him.

The letter to the Hebrews says of Jesus that 'he has been tempted as we are'. In becoming like us, Jesus experienced temptation as we do. None of us are strangers to temptation. If it was a struggle at times for Jesus to remain faithful to God's call, it will certainly be a struggle for us. We will find ourselves pulled in a direction that does not correspond to God's will for our lives. Unlike Jesus, we will sometimes find ourselves taking that direction, going down a path that falls short of what God wants for us. In that sense, the story of Adam and Eve in the garden, which we read in today's first reading, is the story of us all. According to that story, Adam and Eve had great scope to enjoy the goodness of God's creation, but there was a limit. They were tempted to ignore this limit, to reach for something that was out of bounds for them, and they surrendered to that temptation. Their failure to be faithful to what God asked of them stands in sharp contrast to the faithfulness of Jesus in today's gospel reading. St Paul, in today's second reading, reflects on that contrast between Adam and Christ.

If the story of Adam and Eve is very much our story, St Paul would remind us that the story of Jesus can also be our story. We have been baptised into Christ; we receive him in the Eucharist; his Spirit has been given to us. When we are tempted, therefore, we do not stand alone. At such moments, the Lord is present within us and around us, helping us to be faithful to God's will for our lives as he was. The Lord wants to live out his faithfulness to God in each one of our lives; his grace is at work in our lives to enable us to be as faithful to God as he was. Lent is a season when we are called to be less of an Adam figure and more of a Christ figure. It is a time when we consciously strive to allow our lives to be shaped more by the story of Jesus than the story of Adam. In Lent we try to identify the temptations that are most significant for us; we acknowledge honestly the ways in which we have surrendered to such temptations, and we invite the Lord to enter our lives more fully, so that the story of his faithfulness to God's call becomes our story to a greater degree. If that happens for us this Lent, we will stand with confidence to renew our baptismal promises this coming Easter Sunday.

Second Sunday of Lent

If any one of us were to look back over the past number of years of our lives, we would more than likely be able to identify times when life was difficult, and other times when all seemed well. Last Sunday the gospel reading put before us a testing time in the life of Jesus. This Sunday the gospel reading presents us with a very different moment in Jesus' life, when his experience of God calling his name in love left him transfigured.

Many of us might find it easier to identify the wilderness type of experience in our lives. Painful experiences have a way of staying with us long after we have moved on from them. Today's gospel reading, however, invites us to recall the mountain top experiences we may have had. These are the times when, in the words of Peter in today's gospel reading, we said, 'It is wonderful for us to be here.' What was it about his experience on the mountain that made Peter say that? He and the other two disciples saw Jesus in a way they had never seen him before. The glory of God shone through Jesus in a way that had never happened before. On the mountain top they had an experience of God, and that is why Peter said, 'It is wonderful for us to be here.' We could say that they had an experience of heaven. The experience was so wonderful that they did not want to come down the mountain.

The experiences in our own lives that make us say, 'It is wonderful for us to be here', are also going to be, in some way, experiences of God. We will not necessarily have to go up a physical mountain to have such experiences of God. We can be fortunate enough to experience something of God's love in and through the people that cross our path in life. In the response to this morning's psalm we prayed, 'May your love be upon us, O Lord.' The Lord's love can come upon us in and through those we meet. Similarly, something of God's passion for justice and for truth can be revealed to us through people who enter our lives. Whenever we experience those divine qualities of love, justice and truth in others, we may find ourselves saying, 'It is wonderful for us to be here.' God can also touch our lives in ways that do not directly involve other people. Time on our own in the presence of nature can leave us with a deep feeling of wonder and gratitude. Such experiences are ultimately experiences of God.

Jesus spoke of God as the God of the living, not of the dead. Any experience that leaves us feeling more alive is an experience of God. I am sure you could probably think of many such experiences. Whenever we have opportunities to be creative, for example, we generally feel more alive. The most wonderful expression of human creativity is when a man and a woman come together in love and bring forth new life in the form of a child. I can only imagine that to look upon one's newly born child is to feel fully alive. That is surely an experience of God. There are other ways in which people can be creative. A writer creates something with his or her pen, carpenters with their tools, artists with their brushes and paint. When such people create well and look upon what they have created, they invariably feel more alive. Therein lies an experience of God. Others have the gift of helping to create community. People who are involved in bringing others together in ways that nurture them are being very creative. Again, when such people do that well, they feel more alive because of it. That too is, ultimately, an experience of God. We all have the capacity to be creative in some way. If God is the Creator and we are made in God's image, it follows that to be human is to be creative.

Today, we give thanks for all those deeply satisfying experiences in life that anticipate the full experience of God that awaits us beyond this life. We can draw strength from such experiences as we face into the more painful experiences of life, when God can seem absent. God who was present to Jesus on the mount of transfiguration was equally present to him on the hill of Calvary, bringing him through the experience of death to new life. God is present to us in our own Calvary experiences too, even if that presence is less tangible. In the words of today's psalm, we can be assured that the Lord looks on those who hope in his love, to rescue their souls from death.

Third Sunday of Lent

We all meet several people in the course of a day. Some we know well, others are strangers to us. Many of the meetings we have with people do not register greatly with us. Once the meeting has passed, we do not think much about it. Other meetings can linger on in our memories, for various reasons. Some of our meetings with people drain us of energy; others leave us feeling more alive.

During his public ministry, Jesus met with all sorts of people. In the course of some of those meetings, he experienced great openness. Other times he met with rejection and hostility. In today's gospel reading the evangelist tells of an unlikely and unusual meeting between two strangers. It was unlikely because it was a meeting between a Jew and a Samaritan in Samaria and, normally, Jews did not venture into Samaria – no more than Jews today would ramble into Gaza. It was unusual because it was a meeting between a man and a woman in a public place and in that time and culture a man did not address a woman in public, unless she was his wife. This meeting happened because one of the two people wanted it to happen. The woman, initially at least, was a reluctant participant in the meeting. Jesus took the lead to initiate the conversation, and he directed the conversation right to the end. The woman was drawn into a conversation that was not of her making. The meeting was driven by Jesus' desire to bring her and her Samaritan people to recognise him as God's anointed one, the giver of true and enduring life.

The strong initiative that Jesus took to make this unconventional meeting happen shows us something about the Lord's relationship with each one of us. It tells us that the Lord's search for us is always more significant than our search for him. The Lord's desire to meet us is not dependant on our willingness or otherwise to meet him. Most human relationships, if they are to develop at all, require an equal investment from both parties. That is not true of our relationship with the Lord. His investment in us is always greater than our investment in him, and his desire to relate to us is in no way lessened by any lack of desire on our part.

The Lord's meeting with the Samaritan woman tells us something else that is important about how the Lord relates to us. Jesus met this woman on her home ground, Samaritan territory. He conversed with her at a place that was very familiar to her – the town well to which she probably came every day to draw water. He also entered her life as it was, in all its brokenness and imperfection. Here we have in very concrete terms what the evangelist had said in more abstract terms in the first chapter of his gospel, 'the Word became flesh and dwelt among us'. The Lord relates to all of us in this way, from within our own experience. He meets with us on our own turf, as it were. We do not have to get ourselves somewhere, either in the physical sense or in any other sense, for the Lord to meet with us and to engage us. The Lord always gets himself to where we are. We may sometimes be as surprised as the woman was to find him there. The ordinary places that we journey to every day are also the places to which the Lord journeys to meet with us and to grace us.

The Lord's meeting with the woman reveals yet more about his relationship with us. Jesus met the woman at the well, not to ask something of her but to give her something. Although he initially said to her, 'Give me a drink', he immediately went on to speak about what God was offering, the living water that he could give her and that would become within her a spring welling up to eternal life. The Lord meets us because he has something to offer us, not because he wants something from us. As Paul states in the second reading, the love of God has been poured into our hearts through the Holy Spirit which has been given to us. The Lord meets with us to pour the living water of the Holy Spirit into our hearts. He comes to us in order to grace us.

Having been graced by the Lord, the woman went on to grace others, leaving her water jar and evangelising her whole town, bringing the Samaritans to Jesus. In meeting with us to grace us, the Lord thereby empowers us to grace others; in opening ourselves to the Lord's coming we make it possible for others to meet the Lord.

Fourth Sunday of Lent

A colleague said to me recently that he wished that his eyesight was a little bit worse than it was! His eyesight was poor enough to need glasses some of the time, but not bad enough to need glasses all of the time. As a result, he needed to have his glasses with him, without needing to wear them most of the time. For those of us who wear glasses all of the time, life is a little simpler. However, very few people would wish that their eyesight was a little bit worse than it is.

Today's gospel reading puts before us a man who was blind from birth. When Jesus saw him, he simply presumed that the man wanted to see. Without waiting to be approached by him, Jesus took the initiative to cure his blindness, sending him to wash in the pool of Siloam. It is a reasonable assumption that those who are blind want to see, and that those who see imperfectly want to see fully. Yet, while that may be true when it comes to seeing physically, it is not always true when it comes to deeper forms of seeing. Here, the old adage often holds true: 'There are none so blind as those who will not see.' There are certain forms of blindness that we can easily become attached to. We see much less than what is there to be seen, because we only see what we want to see.

The Pharisees in today's gospel story are a good example of this deeper form of blindness. Because Jesus broke the Sabbath law, as the Pharisees understood it, they saw Jesus as a sinner. Even though there was strong evidence to the contrary, they refused to see it. When the man blind from birth, now healed, pointed to the evidence and said to them, 'If this man were not from God, he could do nothing', they threw him out, declaring that he too, like Jesus, was a sinner. Here was a group who refused to see. Yet, they repeatedly say in the course of the story, 'We know', 'We see'. They were blind to their own blindness. For this reason, Jesus' last words to them were, 'Since you say, "We see", your guilt remains.' It turns out that they are the real sinners, not Jesus or the man born blind.

Our insight into people and into situations is, of necessity, limited, because we are human. The first reading declares: 'God does not see as humans see. Humans look at appearances, but the Lord looks at the heart.' Our seeing will always be, to some extent, a superficial seeing. Because our ability to see others is so limited, the judgements we make about them on the basis of that seeing will often be wide of the mark. We need to give each other the freedom to be able to say from time to time, 'I got it wrong. There was more there than I saw at the time.' There is a tendency nowadays to devour people, especially those in public life, who admit to having made a wrong judgement. Surely what really matters is not making a wrong judgement, but having the honesty to admit the wrong judgement and the desire to learn from it. At the end of the gospel reading Jesus declares that blindness itself is no sin. The real sin consists in being blind, while persistently claiming, 'We see.'

Immediately after receiving the gift of physical sight from Jesus, the man was still somewhat blind to Jesus' true identity, referring to him simply as 'the man called Jesus'. It was only over time that he came to see Jesus as Lord and deserving of worship. Although initially blind to Jesus' full identity, he remained open to seeing more, to growing in his relationship with Jesus. We too will often find ourselves blind to the true identity of others. We may have been brought up to think of someone or of a whole community in a certain way. What matters is that we acknowledge our blindness in regard to others. Then we will be open to learning more about them, to being shown more. We will be willing to take whatever steps are necessary to move from a very limited perspective on them to a much fuller one.

If there is more to the other than meets the eye, this is supremely the case with Jesus, of whom the fourth evangelist said, 'the world itself could not contain the books that could be written' about him. In his regard, we can never claim to see fully. The blind man's willingness to set out on a journey of coming to know Jesus more fully, in spite of the hostility of others, is an inspiration for us all.

Fifth Sunday of Lent

As the days get longer and the signs of growth in nature become more obvious, we can begin to feel that winter is loosening its grip on us. The signs of new life in nature are the promise of more to come. As nature begins to come alive again, many people also feel more alive at this time of the year. The longer evenings call us forth, and we find ourselves doing more walking than we have done for some months.

Yet, not everyone will be feeling more alive in these early days of spring. Those who have been recently bereaved will be feeling drained of life and energy. They may feel that a part of themselves has died, and that in a very real sense they are less alive now. Others among us may be feeling drained of life for a host of other reasons. Some may be struggling with some kind of illness; others may be trying to cope with an experience of rejection or disappointment; some may be struggling with an experience of personal failure; others may be overworked and over-tired. For a variety of reason, as individuals, as families, as a community, we can be feeling less alive than we want to be and are capable of being.

In today's gospel reading, a family who were struggling with the serious illness of one of their members sent to Jesus, their friend, for help, 'He whom you love is ill.' By the time Jesus arrived, this family's struggle with serious illness had given way to the more life-draining struggle with death. The message to Jesus now was, 'If you had been here, my brother would not have died.' We can sense in that statement the family's anguish, disappointment and, even, anger. Yet, Jesus entered fully into their deep grief, and went on to call Lazarus out of his tomb, bringing him from death to life, and his family from darkness to light. In doing so, he revealed himself as the resurrection and the life.

When Jesus said to Martha, 'I am the resurrection and the life', he immediately went on to ask her, 'Do you believe this?' The evangelist intends that the readers of his gospel would hear this question as addressed to them. We are each asked to believe that Jesus is the resurrection and the life for us, and that he has the power to call us out of our tombs, to lead us from death to life. Those words of Jesus have given many of us hope in the face of the death of loved ones. We trust that our loved ones who have believed in Jesus will live beyond death; we believe that we ourselves, in virtue of our relationship with Jesus, already live with a life that physical death will not diminish or, much less, destroy.

Yet, we also believe that the Lord who calls us out of the tomb of physical death is also calling us out of other tombs we may have built for ourselves. In the first reading, the Lord, speaking through the prophet Ezekiel, says: 'I mean to raise you from your graves, my people, and lead you back to the soil of Israel.' The grave or the tomb in question was the tomb of exile in a foreign land. In the second reading, St Paul mentions that our body may be dead because of sin. Certain lifestyles can entomb us, and drain us of life. The choices we make as individuals can damage and diminish us, both physically and spiritually. The Lord is constantly calling us out of our various tombs, out of those situations that diminish us and that rob us of what St Paul calls the glorious freedom of the children of God.

In calling people out of their tombs, the Lord looks to us to help him in this work. When Jesus came to the tomb of Lazarus, he called on people to 'Take the stone away', and then to 'Unbind him, let him go free.' The Lord involved others in his life-giving work. He looks to us today to be channels of his life-giving presence to others. Today's gospel challenges us to be life-givers in a world where the taking of life has become much more common than it used to be. We might reflect today on what the Lord's words in the gospel reading could mean for each of us concretely – 'Take the stone away', 'Unbind him, let him go free.' If the Spirit of God has made his home in us, as the second reading states, we cannot underestimate our capacity to be life-givers for others. There is some life-giving work that, with the Lord's help, we can do for others, and which, if we do not do it, may never get done.

Palm Sunday

They say that a week is a long time in politics. Politicians who are in positions of responsibility at the beginning of a week can find themselves out of a job by the end of the same week. A week can be a long time in any of our lives. The situation that we find ourselves in at the beginning of a week can be very different from how things might stand with us at the end of the same week. The awareness of this leads many people to live life one day at a time, living each day well and to the full as it comes along.

It is hard to conceive of a greater contrast than that between the beginning and the end of Jesus' final week. The gospel that we read at the beginning of Mass tells us that the crowds welcomed Jesus into Jerusalem with great enthusiasm, declaring God's blessings on the one who came in the name of the Lord. According to the second gospel reading this morning, by the end of that week, the same crowds were crying out, 'Crucify him'. Jesus who entered Jerusalem on a donkey to a great welcome was carried out of the city as a dead man a few days later, having suffered the cruellest form of death that the Roman Empire could devise.

The people of Jerusalem who welcomed Jesus into their city did not know how the week would end. We who take up our palm branches this morning and who identify with the welcoming crowd know well how the week will end. We also know that the death of Jesus on a Roman cross was not really how this week ended. As Paul reminds us in today's second reading, Christ 'was humbler yet, even to accepting death, death on a cross. But God raised him high.' We are beginning a long week in the church's year, 'Holy Week'. This week takes us from the tumultuous welcome extended to Jesus when he entered Jerusalem, through the deep darkness of his passion and death, and onto the wonderful event of his triumph over death in the resurrection, a triumph in which we all share. There is much to ponder this coming week.

People tend to be busier now than they have ever been. We seem to have more to do and less time to do it. This Sunday we might resolve to slow down a little this coming week so as to allow the momentous events that we are celebrating in the church to touch our hearts and minds. The core of this Holy Week is what we call the Easter Triduum, which begins with the celebration of the Eucharist on Holy Thursday evening and concludes with the Easter Vigil on Holy Saturday night. This short time from the evening of Holy Thursday to Holy Saturday night is the most sacred time in the church's year. It is sacred because during it we celebrate what has been called 'the work of our redemption'.

We have just heard the story of Jesus' passion and death according to Matthew. As we begin this holy week, we are given a preview of where this week is heading. Although we use the term 'passion' with reference to the suffering of Jesus, in normal day to day usage the term refers to a strong feeling or a strong commitment. We all have a passion in that sense. The term can be readily applied to Jesus in this same sense. He suffered his passion, because he had a great passion, a passion for God and for humanity. He died because he was passionately devoted to revealing God's love for all. In taking the cup of wine at the last supper, Jesus said, 'This is my blood, the blood of the covenant, which is to be poured out for many, for the forgiveness of sins.' Jesus' death reveals God's passionate love, a love that is stronger than sin, no matter how grave. When Jesus spoke of his blood poured out for 'many', the many included those who were responsible for his death; it includes all of us here in the church this morning.

We approach this Holy Week with reverence because we know that the last journey of Jesus was one that he travelled for all of us. We are not simply spectators at an event that happened a long time ago. We tell this story every year because it is our story. It is the ongoing story of God's reaching out to us through his Son. Jesus poured out his life for us in love, so that we might pour out our lives in love for him and for each other. Let the palms we take home today be a sign of our desire to do just that.

Holy Thursday

We can learn a lot from the way that children express·their faith. Those of us who are adults tend to think of ourselves as the children's teachers. Yet, they can teach us a lot, especially when it comes to our relationship with God. Their spontaneous openness to the Lord when they are very young can touch our own faith and help to deepen it.

On one occasion in the gospel story the disciples of Jesus were trying to block parents from bringing their children to Jesus. They were clearly of the view that children should be neither seen nor heard. The evangelist tells us that Jesus was indignant with his disciples and said to them, 'Let the children come to me; do not stop them ... Truly I tell you, whoever does not receive the kingdom of God like a little child will not enter it.' Jesus was saying to his disciples, 'Look at the children and learn from them. They have a lot to teach you about receiving the gift of the kingdom of God.' Children know how to receive the gift of God. Their openness to the gift of God can help to open up all of our hearts to the Lord's presence and call in our own lives.

The meaning of Holy Thursday could be summed up in that word 'gift'. At the last supper Jesus gave his disciples the gift of himself in loving service. He did this in two ways. Firstly, he washed their feet, a menial task that servants in a household usually performed. In washing the feet of his disciples, Jesus was showing that he was their servant, our servant. We usually think of Jesus as Lord. 'Jesus is Lord' is one of the great Christian confessions. How can a Lord do the work of a servant? This was why Peter objected to what Jesus was doing – 'You will never wash my feet.' Peter, unlike children, could not receive the gift of Jesus' service. However, Jesus was showing by this gesture that he exercises his lordship not by ruling and dominating but by serving, by giving the gift of himself. It was by giving the gift of himself to us that he became our Lord. In laying down his garments to wash the feet of his disciples, Jesus was anticipating the greater gift he would give them the following day, when he would lay down his life for them and for us on the cross.

The second way that Jesus gave the gift of himself to his disciples at that last supper was by giving himself to them under the form of bread and wine. Taking bread, he blessed it and gave it to them saying, 'Take and eat.' Taking a cup of wine, he blessed it and gave it to them saying, 'Take and drink.' Like the washing of their feet, that gift of himself under the form of bread and wine anticipated the gift of himself that he would make to them and to all of us the following day on the cross. In allowing Jesus to wash their feet and in taking the bread and the cup, the disciples were receiving the gift of himself that Jesus would give them from the cross. In receiving that gift they would never be the same again. They would now have to give as they had received.

Jesus intended that what happened at the last supper would be the shape of the church forever, the shape of our own lives. The last supper was not just a once off event. When he had washed feet of his disciples, he said to them, 'Do as I have done … love one another as I have loved you.' As he has served us, we are to serve one another, and in serving one another, the Lord continues to serve us in and through each other. In giving the bread and cup to his disciples he said to them, 'Do this in memory of me.' We are to repeat the words and actions over the bread and cup, and in doing that the Lord will continue to give himself to us under the form of bread and wine. This is what we do when we celebrate the Eucharist. Both of those commands that Jesus gave at the last supper are important: 'Love one another as I have loved you', and 'Do this in memory of me.' A life of service and the celebration of the Eucharist are both at the heart of what it means to be the Lord's followers. At the Eucharist we receive again the Lord's gift of himself that he made to us on the cross, and in receiving that gift we find the strength to live faithfully the call to serve one another as he has served us.

Good Friday

We have just heard the story of the passion and death of Jesus according to John. It is only this evangelist who gives us the long dialogue between Jesus and Pilate, in the course of which Jesus declares, 'Yes, I am a king. I was born for this, I came into the world for this; to bear witness to the truth.' Jesus came into the world to bear witness to the truth, according to this evangelist, and it was because of his witness to the truth that he was crucified. Jesus witnessed to the truth by speaking the truth about God and about himself. There was no pretence in him; he did not try to hide who he was or who God is. As he says to the high priest in the story we have just heard, 'I have spoken openly for all the world to hear ... I have said nothing in secret.' Prior to that, when the arresting party had come to the garden of Gethsemane looking for Jesus of Nazareth, Jesus declared openly, 'I am he.' Witnessing to the truth, making God fully known, and making himself known as God in human form, proved to be a very dangerous business for Jesus; it led him to his death on a cross.

In contrast to Jesus who witnessed to the truth, the story we have just heard portrays Peter as someone who tried to hide the truth. Twice when it was put to him that he was one of Jesus' disciples, he said 'I am not.' In contrast to Jesus' 'I am', there stands Peter's 'I am not.' Peter denied the truth about himself so as to avoid the painful consequences of witnessing to the truth. Jesus and Peter are a study in contrast. Yet, we find it easy to feel sympathy for Peter because we recognise something of ourselves in him. Like him, we too can struggle to witness in any public way to our relationship with the Lord.

Jesus did not give up on Peter when Peter failed to witness to the truth of who he was. After he was raised from the dead, he appeared to Peter and asked him three times, 'Do you love me?' – giving Peter the opportunity to renew his relationship with the Lord. The Lord repeatedly gives us the same opportunity whenever we fail. The Lord's love is faithful. That is the truth that Jesus came to witness to. He witnesses to a love that is stronger than sin and death, to a God who so loved the world that he gave and continues to give his only Son. That is why we call this day Good Friday. That is why on this day every year we gather at three o' clock in the afternoon to venerate the wood of the cross. In some way we want to respond to the Son of God who, in the words of St Paul, loved me and gave himself for me.

As Christians we do not look upon the wood of the cross primarily as an instrument of torture. Rather, in the words of today's second reading, we look upon it as the throne of grace where we can be assured of finding mercy. It is the fourth evangelist who, more than any of the other evangelists, portrays the cross of Christ as the throne of grace. In this gospel, the cross is, as it were, bathed in a heavenly light, the light of God's love. Here is the light that shines in the darkness and that the darkness cannot overcome, as the prologue to the fourth gospel stated. It can be hard in life to find a love that is strong, that stands firm, irrespective of what is thrown at it. We find such a strong love on Calvary. This is the truth that Jesus witnessed to, by his life, and especially by his death.

We gather here this afternoon to venerate this strong love but also to allow ourselves to be changed by it. The evangelists all suggest that several people were changed for the better by their presence on Calvary that afternoon. One such person is Nicodemus who features only in John's gospel. His initial approach to Jesus was very tentative, coming to him under cover of darkness. After Jesus was lifted up on the cross, however, Nicodemus finally came out into the light, publicly associating himself with Jesus, arranging with Joseph of Arimathea that Jesus would have a burial fit for a king. In venerating the cross this afternoon we too are being called to step more fully into the light, to express our relationship with Jesus more publicly, more generously, more courageously. We are sent out from here as witnesses to the truth, to Jesus who is the way, the truth and the life.

Easter Vigil

Easter is a feast that encourages us to look for new beginnings in what appear to be dead ends. Easter teaches us to expect to find signs of new life at the very moment when all seems lost. In tonight's gospel reading the women went to the tomb expecting a meeting with death. Instead they were met by an angel who declared that the one who was crucified had risen. God had taken everyone by surprise – the Roman guards, the women and the other disciples. The gospel reading says that the women were 'filled with awe and great joy'. God had completely shattered the women's expectations. In raising his Son from the dead, God had done immeasurably more than all they could have asked for or imagined. In the words of Paul's first letter to the Corinthians, 'eye has not seen, nor ear heard, nor the human heart conceived what God has prepared for those who love him'. To everyone's amazement on that Easter morning, God brought surprising new life out of the place of death.

Easter reveals and celebrates a God who is in love with life, a God who continually brings new life out of all our deaths, who is constantly at work to turn our tombs into signs of hope and places of fresh life. Easter teaches us that, because God is at work among us, even our most bitter disappointments can contain the seeds of new beginnings and even our most painful experiences can be life-giving for ourselves and for others. We have all shared to some extent in that sad journey of the women to the tomb in the half-light. These are the experiences that can leave us drained of life, of energy and of enthusiasm. They can take many forms – the pain of bereavement, the anguish of personal failure, a decline in health and mobility, a breakdown in a significant friendship, a loss of job or position. Easter assures us that God can work powerfully even in such dark places. To our amazement, we can discover, as the women did, that what we thought of as a tomb becomes a well-spring of new life. God is constantly at work in our lives bringing life out of death, transforming seeming dead-ends into doorways to life. Easter, in that sense, is not just a past event. It is happening now, because the God who raised Jesus from the dead is actively at work in all our lives, in our personal lives, our communal life, in the life of our church and of our world. Because the God of Easter is at work among us, we are an Easter people, a hopeful people, who recognise that God's life-giving presence is stronger than sin and death.

We will often find that our hope-filled faith in a God of life can be difficult to sustain in the world in which we live. The harsh winds of cynicism, pessimism and negativity can threaten to extinguish our flame of hope. Continuing human cruelty can undermine our faith in God's capacity to work in any kind of life-giving way. Indeed our conviction about God powerfully at work in the midst of suffering and loss will be dismissed as pure nonsense by some. In our own time we continue to hear the voice of those who went to Pilate declaring, 'Command the tomb to be made secure', and who were given a detachment of guards to ensure the tomb stayed closed. Tonight, the risen Lord comes to us in this special celebration to rekindle our hope in his power to open our tombs; he comes to renew our conviction about his life-giving presence at the heart of all things, even at the heart of darkness.

In tonight's gospel reading, the women who were filled with joy by their surprising discovery were sent out by the risen Lord as messengers of Easter hope and joy to the other disciples, whom the Lord identifies as his brothers and sisters. The women's journey away from the tomb was very different from their journey to the tomb. They came to the tomb immersed in their own grief, intending to mourn the dead; they left the tomb as messengers of the risen Lord, as apostles to the disciples. The risen Lord who comes to us on this Easter night calls us and empowers us to take a new path, a path that goes out towards others, that is in the service of those whom the Lord calls his brothers and sisters. The Lord who is powerfully at work in our lives sends us out as messengers of hope to each other, especially to those who have lost heart and hope. We are to announce that the Lord is going ahead of us into all the places we are journeying towards; we will see him there.

Easter Sunday

When people start to run it can indicate any number of things. They may be running because they are rushing for some appointment or they may be in a hurry to get away as quickly as possible from some dangerous situation. Others run out of a sense of excitement, as when people who are close to each other and who have not seen each other for years run towards each other when they meet up again.

The running that we find in the gospel reading this morning comes into this last category. Mary Magdalene came to the tomb of Jesus to grieve there. To her great surprise, she discovered that the stone had been rolled away from the entrance to the tomb and the body of Jesus was no longer there. In her excitement she ran to Simon Peter and the beloved disciple. In their excitement, they ran to the tomb together, with the beloved disciple outrunning Peter. The gospel reading captures the excitement of that morning. Expectations had been shattered.

Initially the finding of Jesus' empty tomb left his followers puzzled. Mary Magdalene thought the body had been stolen. Only the beloved disciple understood the true significance of the empty tomb: 'He saw and believed.' The other disciples understood the true meaning of the empty tomb only when the risen Lord appeared to them. Then they understood that the one who had been crucified had been raised from the dead. Jesus had been wonderfully transformed. Because of this, Jesus' followers were also wonderfully transformed. From being a fearful group who had given up on Jesus' mission, they became joyful, courageous preachers of the good news, declaring that in the life, death and resurrection of Jesus, God was powerfully at work among us.

Resurrection is ultimately about transformation. Jesus who was transformed through being raised to new life holds out the possibility of transformation, not just for his original followers, but for all of us who turn to him in faith. St Paul in his letter to the Philippians declares that the risen Lord will transform our humble bodies into copies of his own glorious body. What God has done for Jesus, God will do for all those who believe in Jesus. It is because of that first Easter Sunday that we can face our own death and the death of our loved ones with great hope. Easter Sunday does not preserve us from the experience of Good Friday. However, it assures us that Good Friday is never the final act in our life's drama. Death does not have the last word. The God of the living will bring us through death to a new and transformed life.

The resurrection of Jesus holds out the possibility of transformation within our earthly lives as well as beyond them. After the death of Jesus, the disciples had lost all heart. The idealism and enthusiasm they first had when they set out to follow Jesus had disappeared. The two disciples on the road to Emmaus provide a good picture of the mood of the disciples after Good Friday. We can all find ourselves in the same place as those two disciples. The difficult experiences of life can drain away our idealism and our enthusiasm. A sense that God has let us down or that God has not answered our prayers can undermine our faith, and cause us to turn away from God. When life goes against us, the temptation to drift into discouragement and disillusionment can be very strong.

The feast of Easter makes it possible for us to resist that temptation. The risen Lord continues to meet with us as he met with the disciples on the road to Emmaus. He continues to call us by name as he called Mary Magdalene by name; he continues to breath the Holy Spirit into our lives as he breathed the Spirit upon the disciples who had locked themselves into a room out of fear; he continues to reveal himself to us in the breaking of bread at the Eucharist. The risen Lord continues to meet us to renew and transform us.

We need to give the risen Lord the opportunity to accomplish his transforming work in our lives. Like Mary Magdalene in today's gospel reading, we need to seek the Lord. We can be sure that in seeking the Lord, he will come to us, as he came to Mary Magdalene. In coming to meet us, he will then call on us to become messengers of Easter joy and hope. He will call on us to share in his life-giving work. The Lord wants to work through us today to bring the light of God's love into the dark corners of our world. That is our Easter mission, our baptismal calling, which we take up afresh this Easter Sunday.

Second Sunday of Easter

We all know from our own experience that liturgical time does not always resonate with where we are on our own life's journey. In the words of today's second reading, we can find ourselves being plagued by all sorts of trials in the season of Easter as much as in any other season. The circumstances of our own lives can make it very difficult for us to sing the Easter Alleluia with any conviction. There is always going to be some tension between the Easter cry, 'Christ is risen! Life has triumphed over death!', and our own present experience. Even though we are an Easter people, we never stop being a Good Friday people also, at least on this side of eternity. We can sometimes find it difficult to believe in the ultimate triumph of life over death, of joy over sadness, especially during those times in our lives when death and sadness become very palpable realities for us.

Perhaps, therefore, we will find it easy to identify with Thomas in today's gospel reading. He had been through the darkness of Good Friday, with all its pain, confusion and disillusionment. When the other disciples approached him with the good news of Easter, 'We have seen the Lord', their message did not resonate with him in any way. The darkness of Good Friday was still too real for him and prevented him from being moved by the Easter proclamation of the other disciples. His own reasoning did not allow him to believe that life had triumphed over death, that the crucified Jesus was now the risen Lord. Thomas stood in the light of Easter, yet that light did not dispel his darkness. In that respect, he may be like many other disciples today. Many believers can be troubled by their sense that the light of Easter does not seem to have penetrated their lives sufficiently. They can be distressed at the degree of doubt that they experience within themselves, troubled that such doubts can become more pronounced as they get older. Like Thomas, they may find it difficult to identify fully with those believers who acclaim with conviction, 'We have seen the Lord', and whose faith seems so much more assured than theirs.

Such people can take heart from today's gospel reading. Indeed, we can all take heart from it, because there is something of Thomas in all of us. The prayer of one of the more minor gospel characters, 'Lord, I believe, help my unbelief', finds a ready place in most of our hearts. Today's gospel reading assures us that the Lord understands a doubting, questioning, faith. When the Lord appeared to Thomas, he did not rebuke him. He accommodated himself to Thomas's demand to touch his wounds, before calling on him to 'doubt no longer but believe'. Then, out of the mouth of the great sceptic came the fullest profession of faith in the fourth gospel, 'My Lord and my God.' The evangelist is perhaps indicating to us that both serious doubt and great faith can reside in one and the same person.

Thomas, like the other disciples, saw and believed. However, the Lord recognises that only a small group of disciples will see and believe and, so, he speaks a beatitude to the many future disciples who will believe without seeing. That beatitude embraces all of us gathered here this morning. As Peter puts it in today's second reading, 'You did not see him, yet you love him.' The church is the community of those who believe in and love the Lord, without having seen the Lord. We look forward to that day when we will see the Lord, face to face. Because we do not yet see him face to face, our faith is always a faith that hopes. To believe is always at the same time to wait in joyful hope.

The risen Lord's face to face meeting with Thomas dispelled all Thomas's doubts. Because we only live in hope of such a meeting, there will always be some element of doubt in our own faith. As Paul says in his first letter to the Corinthians, 'now we see as in a mirror, dimly'. The questioning of our reason that is an inevitable part of seeing dimly is not an enemy of faith. It can lead, rather, to a deepening of our faith. If we face our questions honestly, as Thomas did, and bring them to each other and to the Lord, we too can find ourselves exclaiming, 'My Lord and my God.' In one of his encyclicals, *Faith and Reason*, Pope John Paul II stated that 'the church remains profoundly convinced that faith and reason mutually support each other ... they offer each other a purifying critique and a stimulus to pursue the search for a deeper understanding'.

Third Sunday of Easter

Many of us will have experienced deep loss, with the death of a close relative or a good friend. Life after such a loss can be very difficult. There are other kinds of losses that we experience in the course of our lives, such as the loss of a job, or the loss of full health, or the loss of our good name. All of these experiences of loss are life-draining and debilitating.

When we are struggling with some experience of loss, we need the support of others who are going through this experience with us. People who are going through a similar grieving experience can give great strength to each other. That is what we find happening at the beginning of today's gospel reading. Two grieving disciples walk along together. The one whom they had been following, and in whom they had put so much hope, had been crucified by the Romans. They were in the throes of deep grief. As the gospel reading says, their faces were downcast. These two disciples were supporting each other in their grief. As they walked along together, they were telling each other the story of what happened in recent days. Those who have been through an experience of loss know how therapeutic it can be to tell the story of the last days of a loved one. Telling the story helps us to come to terms with what has happened. Putting words on the events that have caused us such grief can help us to find some meaning in what has happened.

Having told the story to each other, the two disciples told it to the stranger who joined them on the road. The story they told was a true story but it was not the whole story. Theirs was a story about a great prophet who said and did wonderful things, who had been unjustly put to death, and whose body had gone missing from the tomb. The stories we tell each other can often be like that. They reveal a certain insight into what has happened, but very often a limited insight. We can make the mistake of thinking that how we talk about something is all that there is to it. In reality, if the event in question is a complex and significant one, especially if it is somewhat mysterious, there are many stories that could be told about it. Our story, the way we talk about it or write about it, is only one way of putting it. If we become too attached to our way of telling the story, we can become blind to other ways of seeing and of understanding what has happened. This can happen all too easily, as we know. What is important is that we allow the particular story that we tell to be enriched by the very different story about the same events that people who may be strangers to us have to tell.

That is one way of understanding what is happening on the road to Emmaus in today's gospel reading. When the two disciples told their story of the recent events in Jerusalem, the stranger who had joined them and who had listened carefully to their story told another story about those same events. Whereas the story of the two disciples was one which ended in death and confusion, the stranger told a very different story, one that contained the story of the two disciples but brought it much further. The stranger's story ended not in death but in glory. 'Was it not ordained', he asked, 'that the Christ should suffer and so enter into his glory?' As the stranger told his story, something happened within the two disciples. In their own words, their hearts burned within them. They began to see that there was more to what had happened than they realised; this stranger was giving them a whole new understanding of what they had come to see as an awful tragedy. They wanted more; they asked him to stay, and over table they recognised him in the breaking of the bread. Then their eyes were opened, and the sad journey away from Jerusalem became a joyful journey back to the city.

The story of the stranger can have a lot to say to us. We need to listen to the strangers in our midst. In today's gospel reading, the stranger is the risen Lord. The risen Lord's story continues to speak powerfully to us today. The sad stories we often tell each other need to be exposed to the light of the Lord's story. If we listen to that story, if we are attentive to the word of the Lord, we will begin to recognise life where we thought there was only death, light where we had seen only darkness.

Fourth Sunday of Easter

Gates have become more of a feature of our urban landscape. New upmarket housing blocks tend to be gated affairs. Certainly, one purpose of a gate is to prevent access to some area. Another purpose of a gate, however, is to provide access to an area. The large gates you find in our rural landscape come to mind. A gate creates an opening into an otherwise closed environment.

It is in this latter sense that we have to understand the reference to the gate in this morning's gospel reading. The sheepfold mentioned in the gospel reading was an enclosed area. The gate of the sheepfold provided access both into and out of the enclosure, enabling the sheep to pass out of the enclosure to green pasture and to come back into the enclosure again for safety and protection. Jesus identifies himself as the gate in this sense. As the gate, all who enter through him will be safe; as the gate, all who exit through him will find pasture. He sums up this twofold role he has as the gate by affirming, 'I have come so that they may have life and have it to the full.' The purpose of all that Jesus said and did is that we might have life, and have it in abundance.

Just as the gospel reading is clear about why Jesus has come, it is also clear about what we must do. If we are to come into that abundant life that Jesus came to give us, we must do so by passing through him. We are to take Jesus as our gate, going 'freely in and out' through him, as the gospel reading puts it. Jesus uses many images of himself in John's gospel. Many of those images stress what Jesus does for us. As the good shepherd, for example, Jesus lays down his life for us. The image of Jesus as the gate emphasises more what we must do in response to all that Jesus has done and is doing for us. If Jesus is the gate that leads to abundant life, we have to choose to pass through that gate. No one can do that for us. The presence of a gate does not automatically mean that people will use it.

We are more aware today than in the past that our relationship with Jesus and with his followers is a choice we have to make. There is no longer a strong current flowing in the direction of Jesus that will carry us along. Indeed, it could be argued that the current is flowing in the opposite direction. The messages that we receive from the culture in which we live are not ones that have been strongly shaped by the values that Jesus embodied in his life, death and resurrection. There are a whole variety of gates opening up to us, beckoning us to pass through. If we are to pass through the gate that is Jesus, we have to consciously choose this gate and exclude other gates. When Peter preached the gospel to the crowd in Jerusalem, their response was to ask Peter, 'What must we do?' They understood that the gospel they had heard placed an onus on them to make choices they had never made before. The question 'What must we do?' is as valid a question for us today, as it was for the people of Jerusalem two thousand years ago. Every day we try to discern what we need to do to give expression to our desire to take Jesus as our gate.

Yet, the gospel reading this morning assures us that in trying to answer the question, 'What must we do?', we are not thrown back on our own resources alone. We are not left to ourselves in trying to distinguish the gate that is Jesus from the many other gates that lead in different directions. The parable that Jesus tells in the gospel reading makes reference to a shepherd as well as to a gate. He is both the gate and the shepherd. Our going through the gate is always in response to the call of the shepherd. Indeed, the shepherd leads us through the gate. One by one, according to the gospel reading, he calls his own and leads them out. The shepherd calls out to each of us individually, by name. Today, vocations Sunday, reminds us that we all have a vocation in that very fundamental sense. Jesus' call comes to us in all kinds of ways. Sometimes, we hear that call more loudly than at other times. Today, we pray that we would listen more attentively to the call of the good shepherd, so that we may choose Jesus as our gate on our journey through life.

Fifth Sunday of Easter

Most of us do not like conflict and try to avoid it. Yet, we know from our experience that some element of conflict is inevitable in life. We often struggle to know how best to resolve the conflict. If we say nothing, resentment and anger can build up within us. If we say too much, we can make a bad situation worse. A third party can be a great help in enabling the conflict to be resolved in a way that is in everyone's best interest.

In today's first reading we hear of a situation of conflict in the early church. The Hellenists, or Greek-speaking Jewish Christians, made a complaint against the Hebrews, or Aramaic-speaking Jewish Christians. There was tension between two language groups, with one group feeling that their more vulnerable members, the widows, were being neglected. We know that there is more to language than just a set of words. Any language expresses a certain outlook on the world, embodies a particular culture. Even from its earliest days, the church was multi-cultural. There was always the potential for one group to feel that the other group were being better served. A third party helped to resolve the conflict mentioned in that first reading. The twelve apostles stepped up and showed the kind of leadership needed to resolve the developing conflict. They asked the church to call forth from among themselves more leaders to serve the community. The twelve recognised that the burden of service needed to be carried by a greater number of people. A small group of people, like the twelve, could not do everything well. If the twelve were to devote themselves to the ministry of prayer and of the word, others needed to take responsibility for other ministries, such as the ministry of hospitality and of attending to the physical welfare of the needy. When this happened, the reading states that 'the number of disciples in Jerusalem was greatly increased'.

In every age the church has to face the same kind of issues that we find the early church struggling with in the first reading. In any parish community there will be tensions similar to those present in the church of Jerusalem. Some groups or some individuals in a parish can often feel that they are being neglected. There are a whole variety of ways in which people need to be served within a parish community. If this is to happen, the burden and the privilege of service has to be shared by a large number of people. We need parishes in which everyone's gifts are called forth and placed at the service of others in the community. The twelve apostles realised that they had an important contribution to make to the community, offering it the ministry of prayer and of the word. They also realised that there were other services that they could not provide. They were confident that the Holy Spirit would equip other people for these other tasks of service. We can have the same confidence today.

Today's first reading encourages us to believe that the Lord will always provide for the needs of the church. The Lord will see to it that there are people, 'filled with the Spirit and with wisdom', available to serve the church in a whole variety of ways. Peter in the second reading reminds all believers that, in virtue of their baptism, they are a holy priesthood, called to offer the spiritual sacrifice of their lives to God and to his people. Peter wants us to take seriously our wonderful baptismal identity, and to be open to the ways in which the Lord is asking us to live out our baptismal calling in service of others. If we each take our baptism seriously and try to live it to the full, the Lord will work powerfully in and through his church.

The encouraging tone of both the first and second reading this morning is heard again in the gospel reading. Jesus turns to his troubled disciples on the eve of his death and says to them, 'Do not let your hearts be troubled. Trust in God still, and trust in me.' At a time when the disciples were struggling with a sense of loss, Jesus speaks of abundance, telling them that there are 'many rooms in my Father's house'. At a time when the disciples feared that the work of Jesus was coming to an end, Jesus tells them that those who believe in him will do even greater works than he has done, because he is going to the Father. These words encourage us to have an expectant faith. The Lord is at work in his church; he is doing a great work and he wants us all to be part of it, in different ways.

Sixth Sunday of Easter

We know from our own experience that we can be closed to some proposal at one moment in our lives and then open to that same proposal at a later moment. We can find ourselves saying 'no' to something, and then, later on, saying 'yes'. We often need time to come around to accepting what we were initially inclined to reject. Most of us admire people who are able to say that they have had another think about something, and in the light of that are now ready to accept what they had dismissed.

According to Luke in his gospel, when Jesus first attempted to preach the gospel to the people of Samaria, they rejected him and his message, because they realised that he was a Jew heading for Jerusalem. The same Luke tells us in today's first reading from the Acts of the Apostles that when Philip went to a Samaritan town and preached the gospel, the Samaritans welcomed the gospel with great joy. Although they had rejected Jesus, they now received his messenger. What Jesus was unable to do in the course of his earthly ministry, the risen Lord accomplished through the ministry of Philip. The Samaritans' initial response to the preaching of the gospel was not to be their final response.

The Lord continued to offer the gospel to those who had initially refused it, and in time, they received it. The story of Jesus' relationship with the Samaritans reminds us that the Lord remains faithful to us, even when we are less than responsive to him. The season of Easter celebrates this faithfulness of the Lord. When the risen Lord appeared to his disciples who had abandoned and denied him, he said to them 'Peace be with you.' The Lord was giving them an opportunity to make a different response to him to the one they had made during the darkness of his passion. Easter celebrates the good news that the Lord's faithfulness is stronger than our faithlessness.

That is why Easter makes us a hopeful people. We are hopeful because we know that, as St Paul puts it in his letter to the Romans, 'nothing in all creation will be able to separate us from the love of God in Christ Jesus our Lord' – not even our own tendency to say 'no' to the Lord. Peter in the second reading calls on believers to always have 'your answer ready for people

who ask you the reason for the hope that you all have'. The hope
that we have does not come from anything in ourselves; it is
rooted in the Lord's faithfulness to us. We are hopeful because
we know that the Lord's 'yes' is always stronger than our 'no'.
Peter tells us in that reading that Christ died for us to lead us to
God. We are confident that the Lord will stop at nothing to lead
us to God, and that is why we are hopeful.

In the gospel reading Jesus assures us that if we do respond
to his initiative towards us, if we strive to love him in response
to his faithfulness to us, then he will give us the Holy Spirit to be
with us forever. When the Samaritans finally made their response to the preaching of the gospel, they experienced the coming of the Spirit into their lives. Their response to the Lord met
with an even greater response to them from the Lord. The Lord
gives generously to all who open their hearts to him. If we turn
to the Lord and seek him, he will give us the gift of the Holy
Spirit. We often associate the giving of the Spirit with the sacraments of baptism and confirmation. These are indeed special
moments when we are given the Spirit, but the gift of the Spirit
is not limited to these moments. The Lord gives us this gift
whenever, like the Samaritans, we respond to the Lord's initiative towards us.

We are only two weeks away from the Feast of Pentecost. In
preparation for this great feast, we might pray each day that
simple prayer, 'Come Holy Spirit, fill the hearts of your faithful.'
In today's gospel reading, the Spirit is spoken of as the Spirit of
Truth. A little later in John's gospel, Jesus says that 'When the
Spirit of Truth comes, he will guide you into all the truth.' The
Lord gives the Spirit as a guide to those who love him. We are
only too well aware of our need of guidance, especially when it
comes to taking the path the Lord wants us to take. The Spirit
will help us to discern where that path lies and will also give us
the courage to take that path. That is why we need to pray,
'Come Holy Spirit'.

The Ascension of the Lord

It can be difficult to appreciate the wonder of a starry sky in the city. The lights of the city prevent us from seeing the sky in all its beauty, even on the clearest of nights. A clear night sky is much more impressive when viewed in the countryside. When you see a night sky in all its clarity you can easily appreciate why the stars have exercised a fascination for people from earliest times. It is understandable why people came to think of the abode of God as somewhere beyond the stars.

In today's first reading, the disciples are asked the question, 'Why are you men from Galilee standing here looking into the sky?' Today's feast of the Ascension is not primarily about the departure of Jesus to some place beyond the stars. Instead, it celebrates the presence of Jesus at the heart of our world. The earthly Jesus was present to a small number of people in a very confined area at a particular moment in human history. The risen Jesus is present to all men and women in every area of the world and throughout all time.

The real meaning of today's feast is well expressed in the promise of the risen Lord to his disciples: 'Know that I am with you always, yes, to the end of time.' The Lord promises to be with his church until the end of time. Earlier in Matthew's gospel, Jesus had spoken the parable of the wheat and the weeds, suggesting that the church was a mixture of the good and the not so good. Jesus understood that his church would always have an ambivalent quality. Something of that ambivalence is evident in the response of the disciples to the risen Lord in today's gospel reading: 'They fell down before him, though some hesitated.' That core group who were to be the nucleus of the church were characterised by a readiness to surrender to the risen Lord and great hesitation before him. The people who make up the church are far from perfect; they are sinners striving to do the will of the Lord. It is this flawed group that the Lord promises to be with until the end of time. We the church need to hear that reassuring promise again and again – especially in those times when as church we are aware that we are not yet all that the Lord is calling us to be.

It was to this ambivalent group that the risen Lord entrusted a most challenging mission: 'Go, make disciples of all the nations, baptise them in the name of the Father and of the Son and of the Holy Spirit, and teach them to observe all the commands that I gave you.' How extraordinary that such a group should be given such a mission. They set out on this mission, not in their own strength, but in the strength of the Lord's promise to be with them until the end of time, and in the power of the Spirit, mentioned in today's first reading. It is because the eleven were faithful to the Lord's call to make disciples of all nations that we are gathered here today in worship. Jesus showed tremendous trust in this rather limited group of disciples. He had faith that, once they were filled with the Spirit, they would work effectively for the coming of the kingdom.

In that sense, the feast of the Ascension celebrates the Lord's faith in his disciples, in us who are his church today. The mission that was given to the first disciples by the risen Lord is given to the church today, flawed as it is. Part of what it means to be a disciple of the Lord is to make other disciples. Parents who bring their children to be baptised are responding to this call of the risen Lord to make disciples of all nations. Jesus states that those who are baptised are to be taught to observe all that Jesus commanded. Those who have been baptised need to be helped to grow in their relationship with the Lord, and the primary location where this happens is the home, not the school or the church building.

Those of us who are not parents are called to make disciples in other ways. In practice, this will often mean supporting those who are already disciples, nurturing their faith, by our prayer, our witness and our service. We are called to support each other, to help each other to become better disciples. This is the wok that the risen Lord entrusts to all of us. As we set about this important work, we draw strength from the Lord's promise to us, 'Know that I am with you always, yes, to the end of time'.

Pentecost Sunday

We have become much more security conscious in recent years. We find it necessary to put locks where there would have been no need for them in the past. We alarm our houses and our cars to a degree that would have been inconceivable a generation ago. This all comes from fear, a fear that is well grounded, as we know only too well. This sense of insecurity and fear can have the negative effect of cutting people off from each other. We can end up retreating beyond our locked gates.

In today's gospel reading, we hear of the disciples locked into a room behind closed doors out of fear. They were terrified that what Jesus' enemies did to him they might also do to them. Circling the wagons was the only strategy they could think of. It needed the risen Lord to appear to them personally for that to change. When he stood among them and said, 'Peace be with you', their fear gave way to joy. When he breathed the Holy Spirit upon them, their retreating behind locked doors gave way to a going forth to preach the gospel to all nations. This is the fourth evangelist's version of Pentecost. He understands it as a moment when the Spirit of the risen Lord drove out the disciples' spirit of fear and isolation. Luke's version of Pentecost, which we find in today's first reading, makes much the same point. The coming of the Spirit on the disciples drove them out of the house in which they were sitting to preach the gospel in a way that was understandable to people of different races and languages.

We can look back on that first Pentecost as the day on which the church was founded, when a fearful group of men and women became, what Paul calls in today's second reading, the body of Christ. However, Pentecost is not simply a past event that was needed to get the church going. The church is always in need of a fresh Pentecost. In his ministry, Jesus encourages us to keep on praying for the coming of the Holy Spirit into our lives. On one occasion he said, 'If you then know how to give good gifts to your children, how much more will the heavenly Father give the Holy Spirit to those who ask him.' We need to keep on praying, 'Come, Holy Spirit.' We are in ongoing need of a fresh Pentecost not only for the church as a whole but also for ourselves as individuals who make up the church. That is why there is a whole range of prayers in the tradition of the church invoking the coming of the Holy Spirit. One such prayer is the Sequence for this Sunday: 'Heal our wounds, our strength renew; on our dryness pour thy dew; wash the stains of guilt away.' This is a prayer that would have sat very easily on the lips of the disciples in today's gospel reading. Those disciples desperately needed the coming of the Holy Spirit and the risen Lord responded to their need. We can be in the same desperate need of the Holy Spirit. One of the ways we can express our need is by praying a prayer similar to what we find in today's Sequence. We can be sure that in praying such a prayer the Lord will not be slow to answer it.

The Holy Spirit came upon the first disciples to renew them, so that they could go forth as the Lord's messengers to others. In a similar way, when the Lord sends the Spirit upon us, he does so with a view to sending us out in service to others. The coming of the Spirit upon us is never for our own benefit alone; it is always with a view to others as well. That is why Paul states in today's second reading that 'the Spirit is given to each person for a good purpose'. As Paul states in that same reading, the coming of the Spirit into our lives enables God to work in us for the service of the Lord. Each of us is born with particular gifts or talents that are natural to us. The Spirit, who comes into our lives in response to our earnest prayer, takes those natural talents and enhances them and gives us a new enthusiasm to use them in the service of the Lord and his people. In that way our natural talents become what St Paul would call charisms. 'There are a variety of charisms', he says in that second reading, 'but always the same Spirit.' Today, we pray for a fresh outpouring of the Spirit upon us so that we may have a new desire and a new energy to do the work of the Lord.

Feast of the Most Holy Trinity

The taking of another person's life is no longer the taboo it once was. We have become accustomed to hearing about the taking of human life on a vicious scale. The taking of a human life is only the most extreme form of eliminating another human being. There are less extreme expressions of that tendency to eliminate others, as when we try to exclude others in some way. Whole communities can exclude other communities with the result that one group within a society can be made to feel like second class citizens. Society can be structured in such a way that large sections of the population can have very restricted access to what others take for granted. As individuals we can exclude people from our lives. When we are angry with people we tend to cut them off. When we perceive them as some kind of a threat we work to keep them at arms length.

Jesus took a strong stance against any form of eliminating others. He not only reiterated the fourth commandment, 'You shall not kill', but he went further and called on his followers not to be angry with others. He rebuked the disciple who drew a sword at the moment of his arrest. He ignored his disciples when in their anger they suggested that they command fire to come down from heaven and consume the Samaritans who had just rejected Jesus. Jesus came not to eliminate or exclude others but to gather them together, to form a new community. The fullest expression of this new human community is what Jesus referred to as the kingdom of God. He had a vision of people coming from east and west, from north and south, to eat together in the kingdom of God. Everything he said and did was shaped by this vision.

Jesus had this vision of a new human community because he understood more than any of us could that God was a community of life. That is what we mean when we speak of God as Trinity. Even thought the term Blessed Trinity is not to be found in the New Testament, the essence of that central teaching of the church is to be found there. In today's second reading, Paul wishes the church in Corinth the grace of the Lord Jesus Christ, the love of God the Father, and the fellowship of the Holy Spirit. Here we find Paul placing God the Father, Jesus the Lord and the Holy Spirit on the same level. Reflecting on all the writings of the New Testament, the church would very soon come to state that the Father is God, Jesus is God and the Holy Spirit is God. God is Father, Son and Holy Spirit. In other words, within God there is a series of loving relationships: the Father loves the Son and the Son loves the Father, and the fruit of that loving relationship is the Holy Spirit who is loved by both. So great is this love within God that it has overflowed to embrace us all. As John says in today's gospel reading, 'God so loved the world that he gave his only Son.' We can add to that and say that God and God's Son so loved the world that they both gave the Holy Spirit. No real community is closed in on itself. The Trinity as the perfect community is certainly not closed in on itself. God the Father, Son and Holy Spirit move towards us to draw us into their wonderful community.

However, we cannot be in communion with the Trinity unless we are striving to be in communion with each other. Jesus who revealed God to us as Trinity calls us to form the kinds of communities that are, to some extent at least, a reflection of the community that is God. That is why the mission of the church in the world is to build community. The mission of each of us as members of the church is to do the same. At its best, a parish is a community of communities. Most of our parishes are too big to have a sense of the parish as a community. However, within any parish there is scope for a number of smaller communities that are linked together. These small communities can take the form of prayer groups, pastoral care groups, justice and peace groups and so on. They might consist in gatherings of people who share a common interest or who are of a similar age range. Many people are giving of their time and energy to make sure that such communities happen. Today's feast of the Trinity is a good day to commit ourselves afresh to this work of forming communities within our parish that reflect the communal life that is God.

The Feast of Corpus Christi

The problem of obesity has been an issue in the developed world in recent times. A lot of concern is being expressed in particular about children who are overweight. Measures are being looked at to encourage children to eat more healthily. In past generations people ate because they were hungry. In the present times there can be a tendency to eat for the sake of eating. This is one of the downsides of relative plenty and prosperity.

In today's first reading, Moses calls on the people to remember the time in the wilderness when they were hungry. They had left Egypt, a land of plenty, and had entered a wilderness where food was scarce. Moses reminded them that in those scarce and lean times, the Lord provided for them. What kept them alive during those lean years was not so much the physical food that was miraculously provided, but rather the Lord who provided that food. There was a lesson here that the people needed to remember when the time of plenty came round again, as it would when they entered the promised land – 'We do not live on bread alone, but on every word that comes from the mouth of God'.

In times of plenty, it is easy to forget that we do not live on bread alone. When there are so many opportunities to satisfy our physical appetites, we can easily loose touch with our deeper appetites. In times when we have the resources to make great material progress, our spiritual progress can suffer. In the Book of Deuteronomy Moses is very aware of this danger and warns the people about it. Jesus was very aware of it too. In commenting on the seed that is choked by thorns, he declares that the lure of wealth and the desire for other things can come in and choke the word. However, neither Moses nor Jesus led a movement into the desert as a way of dealing with the downside of plenty. Both of them stressed that in the midst of plenty we need to remember that we do not live on physical bread alone and to attend to the deeper hungers and thirsts in our lives.

In today's gospel reading, Jesus presents himself as the one who can ultimately satisfy those deeper hungers and thirsts. He is the living bread come down from heaven. It is above all in the Eucharist that Jesus offers himself to us as food and drink for the satisfying of those deeper hungers and thirsts. In coming to the

Eucharist we are opening our hearts to the one who declares that he is the bread of life and who invites us to take and eat. We go to Mass because, in the words of today's gospel reading, 'If you do not eat the flesh of the Son of Man and drink his blood, you will not have life in you.'

It was at the last supper that Jesus first called on his disciples to take and eat, to take and drink, having identified the bread as his body given for them and the wine as his blood poured out for them. At the last supper Jesus gave himself to his disciples as food and drink. At every Eucharist Jesus does the same for subsequent generations of disciples. The feast of Corpus Christi reminds us that the Lord's invitation to take and eat is as strong today as it was two thousand years ago. We come to Mass because, in the words of St Paul in today's second reading, we want to be in communion with the body and blood of Christ, our real food and real drink.

To be in communion with Jesus in the Eucharist is to be in communion with the values that he lived by and died for. When Jesus said to his disciples at the last supper, 'Take and eat', he was at the same time calling on them to stand where he stood, to live out the communion with him they shared at the table after they had left the upper room. However, the communion the disciples shared with Jesus at table was almost immediately shattered as they abandoned him at the moment of his arrest. When we take the bread and the cup of the Eucharist we too are declaring that we want to imbibe all Jesus stood for. We are committing ourselves to live by his values, to walk in his way, to be shaped by his Spirit. We come to Mass not only to receive from Jesus, but also to give to him, to commit to being in communion with him. In that sense, coming to Mass is a serious business. It is making a statement that we will stand with the Lord in all our comings and goings.

Second Sunday in Ordinary Time

When I was a child, if either I or one of my brothers pointed at something, my mother would always say, 'Don't point.' Pointing was considered bad manners, at least for children. There are times, of course, when pointing is considered appropriate. If I am giving someone directions, it can be helpful to point, in order to make clear what I am trying to communicate. You would certainly point to identify a source of danger to yourself and others.

In today's gospel reading, John the Baptist points to Jesus so as to direct people to him. Seeing Jesus coming towards him, John declared: 'Look, there is the Lamb of God who takes away the sin of the world.' Those words of John have become part of our Eucharistic celebration. John's action of physically pointing to Jesus and identifying him as the Lamb of God sums up the meaning of John's life. You could say that John's whole life pointed to Jesus. Indeed, John even pointed his own followers in the direction of Jesus. With reference to Jesus, he said simply, 'He must increase, but I must decrease.' Great as John was, he had the humility to point to someone greater than himself. Pointing to one greater than himself and leading others to this person was the purpose of his life and mission.

Most of us can probably think of people who, in the course of our lives, pointed us in the right direction. These were people who could see just that little bit more clearly than we could at the time. We all need good guides from time to time; we need people who can point the way for us, people who, in the words of Paul's letter to the Philippians, can direct us towards, 'whatever is true, whatever is honourable, whatever is just, whatever is pure, whatever is pleasing, whatever is commendable'. It is true that we can react negatively to people who come across as knowing what is best for us and who take it upon themselves to tell us what to do. However, the art of pointing others in the right direction is more subtle than that. John the Baptist did not say to his disciples, 'Become disciples of Jesus'; he simply said, 'Look, there is the Lamb of God.' Those who point us in the right direction are sharing with us something of their experience and insight. Their sharing serves as an invitation rather than a com-

mand. Such sharing will not always be responded to. Not everyone that John pointed in the direction of Jesus went on to become a disciple of Jesus. The art of pointing others in the right
direction needs to be joined to a profound respect for human
freedom. Today we give thanks for the John the Baptist figures
we have encountered in the course of our lives. We thank God
for all those who were concerned enough about us to share
something of their vision with us, and who remained loyal to us
even when we failed to take the path they pointed out to us.

In thanking God for such people in our lives, we also acknowledge that the Lord calls each of us to become a John the
Baptist for others. Our baptism calls on us to live lives that help
to point others in the direction that God wants them to take. We
cannot become all that God wants us to be on our own; we need
each other. God guides us through others, and guides others
through us. We are dependant on each other if we are to take the
path that leads to God's Son. We can also of course hinder each
other from taking this path. Jesus reserved some of his harshest
words for those who led others astray, those who, in his own
words, 'put a stumbling block before one of these little ones who
believe in me'. Those who lead others astray are at the opposite
end of the spectrum to the likes of John the Baptist.

If we are to become a John the Baptist for others, if we are to
point others in the direction of Jesus, we ourselves need to be
pointing towards Jesus. John could only say, 'Look, there is the
Lamb of God' because he himself knew the Lamb of God. John
admits in today's gospel reading that he only knew Jesus because God had revealed Jesus to him. We too need God to reveal
Jesus to us. We depend on God to bring us into a deeper relationship with Jesus. This is not something we can do for ourselves. We each need to pray, 'Lord God, help me to know your
Son.' Only then can we go on to become a John the Baptist for
others.

Third Sunday in Ordinary Time

There has been a great change in the relationship between the various Christian denominations since the Second Vatican Council. My mother once said of my grandmother that, coming out once from a sermon given at a parish retreat, she turned to my mother, then a young girl, and said, 'God help the poor Protestants.' I suspect that her comments and the understanding behind them were not untypical of the time. Today there is a greater recognition of what the various Christian denominations have in common, and a greater respect for each others' traditions. There is an appreciation that, because of our common baptism, believers of different traditions are already in a significant communion with each other, even if it is partial and incomplete. There is a strong desire to give expression to the communion that does exist between us, such as by praying together, and by working together in practical ways for the coming of God's kingdom.

The source of the unity between Christians of different denominations is the person of Christ. We are all, first and foremost, followers of Christ. St Paul makes this point in today's second reading. He was faced with a church in Corinth that was dividing around different leaders. He wanted believers to move from allegiance to particular leaders to allegiance to Christ. That is why he asked them: 'Was it Paul that was crucified for you? Were you baptised in the name of Paul?' He did not want people saying, 'I belong to Paul.' Christ was crucified for them; they were baptised in the name of Christ; they belong to Christ, not to Paul or to Apollos or to any other human leader. Similarly, in our own time, all Christians, regardless of their tradition, belong to Christ. To the extent that we grow in our relationship with Christ, we will grow in our communion with each other.

The call to conversion, the call to turn towards Christ more fully, is addressed to all Christians. This is the call of Jesus in this morning's gospel reading: 'Repent, for the kingdom of heaven is at hand.' God's kingdom is waiting to happen; God is waiting to rule in our lives. For this to come about we need to keep on turning towards the person of Jesus. This turning towards Jesus is a lifetime's work; it does not happen in an instant. The two sets of brothers in today's gospel reading respond generously to the call of Jesus. However, their initial response was not sustained. In various ways they turned away from the one they set out to follow and, eventually, they abandoned him altogether. They had to be called back again and again to the one they had left everything in order to follow. The initial call, 'repent, for the kingdom of heaven is at hand' is one they needed to hear and respond to over and over again. It was a lifetime's call and a lifetime's response.

It is the same for all of us. We constantly need to turn and return to the person of Jesus, the one into whom we were baptised and whom we desire to follow. Christians of all denominations have to keep on making that journey towards Jesus throughout their lives. It is the willingness and readiness of us all to go on making that journey that will deepen the communion that exists between the different traditions. What is most damaging to that communion is for one group to consider that they have already arrived and that it is everybody else that has to make the journey. We are all pilgrims; we are all on a journey; we are all striving to respond to the Lord's call in the gospel reading, 'Follow me.' We all need to recognise that we often follow other paths and respond to other voices. In that sense we are not yet saved, we have not yet arrived. If anyone asks you, 'Are you saved?' be sure to say 'No.' God's work has not yet been brought to completion in our lives. We are very much God's work in progress, both as individuals and as communities of faith.

God never ceases to work among those who desire to follow his Son. We believe that the Spirit of God, the Holy Spirit, is working to bring all Christians into that unity for which Christ prayed. Christians do not create the movement towards unity; it is always there before us. Our calling is to allow that movement of the Spirit to take flesh in our ways of living and relating to each other. Today, we give thanks for the good work that God has been doing among the followers of his Son, and we pray that we would each in our own way further that work of God in the future.

Fourth Sunday in Ordinary Time

There is a wonderful portrait gallery in London, just around the corner from the National Gallery. There you find portraits of all kinds of people going back over several centuries. The art of portraying someone well on canvas is a very special one. There is more involved in portraying someone well than representing accurately the physical features of the person. A good portrait artist will always capture something of the spirit of the person.

The beatitudes in today's gospel reading could be understood as a portrait of Jesus himself, a kind of self-portrait. They describe his core attitudes and values. He more than anyone else is poor in spirit, trusting in God before all else; he is gentle, in that he is firmly committed to God's purpose, yet without any trace of arrogance; he is the one who mourns because people are not doing what God wants, and who, himself, hungers and thirsts to do God's will; he is merciful to all who are broken in body and spirit; he is pure in heart in that his heart is not divided but is totally given over to the love of God and the service of all God's people; he is the peacemaker who seeks by his life and his death to reconcile all people to God and to each other. He is the one who was prepared to be persecuted in the doing of God's will and in the carrying out of God's purpose.

If the beatitudes are a portrait of Jesus, they are also a portrait of what we are called to become as followers of Jesus. The beatitudes announce that those who live by these attitudes and values of Jesus are blessed because of the future that God has in store for them. It would be a pity to look upon the beatitudes as a lofty ideal that Jesus lived to the full but one that is far beyond us. When Jesus spoke these beatitudes he was looking at men and women like ourselves and he was declaring them blessed because, to some extent at least, they fitted the portrait that he was presenting. We should all be able to find a niche for ourselves somewhere among the beatitudes. In the fourth beatitude, for example, Jesus declares blessed those who hunger and thirst for what is right. This beatitude does not declare blessed those who are *doing* what is right, but those who keep on *striving to do* what God wants, those who hunger and thirst for it. This beatitude acknowledges that doing what God wants is a goal that always lies ahead of us. What matters is that we never cease to strive forward towards that goal, that we do not allow ourselves to become complacent. Even though we repeatedly fall short, as long as we earnestly seek to do what God wants, we are declared blessed, we are congratulated.

The previous beatitude, the third one, refers to those who mourn. Those who hunger and thirst for what is right will invariably be people who mourn, in the sense that they will be aware how far they have yet to go, and that will sadden them. Such people are painfully aware that God's kingdom has not yet come in their own lives or in the society that they inhabit. They mourn over the presence of sin and evil in themselves and in others. The 'mourning' mentioned in the beatitudes is akin to the weeping of Jesus because the people of Jerusalem did not recognise Jesus' ministry as the time when God was visiting them. The difference between the mourning of Jesus and our mourning is that he wept over the sins of others, whereas we need to weep over our own sins as well as those of others. Those who hunger and thirst for what is right will be all too aware of the journey that is yet to be travelled.

Many of us can at least find a niche for ourselves in those two beatitudes. In so far as we belong there, Jesus declares us blessed. In that sense, the beatitudes are a word of encouragement. They can also be a challenging word. To hunger and thirst for what is right is one thing; to be persecuted for what is right is another. That particular beatitude, the eighth one, challenges us to be true to the values of the gospel even if we suffer loss as a result. Sometimes, faithfulness to the Lord will mean taking the road less travelled, going against the tide. We will need the Lord's help if we are to do that, and that brings us to the first beatitude: 'Blessed are the poor in spirit.' Blessed, in other words, are those who recognise their need of God, their dependence on God's help.

Fifth Sunday in Ordinary Time

One of the great compliments that can be paid to someone is to say that he or she is the salt of the earth. We apply that image to those who are decent and kind, who can be relied upon in times of difficulty, and who give generously of themselves to others. Salt tends to get a rather negative press these days. We are told that too much salt is not good for you. Yet, in the world of Jesus, salt was a very precious commodity. It was the primary means of preserving food, and it was used extensively to season food. It is that very positive assessment of salt that is reflected in declaring someone to be 'the salt of the earth'.

In the gospel reading today, Jesus turns to his disciples and says to them, 'You are the salt of the earth.' This group of disciples were the nucleus of what was to become the church. We are the church today, and Jesus, addressing us in today's gospel reading, says to us, 'You are the salt of the earth.' Jesus does not say, 'You are to become the salt of the earth', but 'You *are* the salt of the earth.' We are being reminded of our identity, the identity we share as people who have been baptised into Christ, who are members of Christ's body. It is as if Jesus is saying to us, 'Remember who you are; do not sell yourselves short; take yourselves seriously.'

If that is the identity we share, our calling is to live out of that identity. Like salt, we are to preserve what is best in each other and in our world. Insofar as we bring out the best in others, and nurture all that is good in our midst, we are indeed salt of the earth. Matthew later on in his gospel says of Jesus that he did not break the crushed reed nor quench the smouldering wick. Jesus was careful to nurture and preserve whatever was worthwhile in others, whatever was of God, even if it was barely present. We appreciate people who have that ability to recognise something worthwhile, even if it seems delicate and vulnerable, and who are able to preserve and nurture it. We need such people in our midst if the small seeds that promise so much are to become all they are capable of becoming. Such people encourage and bring out the best in others. We have all known such people.

We may also have met people who belong at the other end of the spectrum, who have a tendency to crush the bruised reed, who seem prone to undermining the good work that is going on within people and between them. The first reading today makes reference to the clenched fist and the wicked word. The clenched fist suggests a hand that is shaped to do damage, to undermine the good that is waiting to be nurtured. As we know, the wicked word can be as undermining as the clenched first. A word of criticism can stifle the good that is struggling to be born in someone. We are all capable both of nurturing the good in others and of undermining whatever may be worthwhile there.

The other image that Jesus uses in the gospel reading is that of light. In John's gospel, Jesus says of himself, 'I am the light of the world.' In Matthew's gospel, he says to his disciples, 'You are the light of the world.' It is striking that a title that is given to Jesus in one gospel is given to us, his disciples, in another. Again, Jesus is reminding us of our identity as those who have been baptised into him and who have been enlightened by his presence in word and sacrament. If salt is associated with preserving, light is associated with showing the way. I dislike driving at night, especially on country roads that have no lighting. It is always a relief to reach a road that is well lit, so that I can see what is ahead, where I am going. Jesus came as light to show us the way, and to walk that way for us and with us. It is the way that was spelt out in the beatitudes in last Sunday's gospel. In today's gospel reading, we are addressed as the light, because we are called to show each other the way, the way of Christ. Our relationship with the Lord is never a purely private affair. We have a responsibility to each other to publicly live that relationship to the full so that we can inspire, guide and lead each other. It is only from each other that we can learn what it means to walk in the way of Christ.

Sixth Sunday in Ordinary Time

We often remark that what is visible is only the tip of the iceberg. We can be very aware that what is hidden is more significant that what is apparent. We may find it difficult to understand why someone behaves in a certain way. Our perplexity can spring from our ignorance of the deeper, invisible, issues that are at the root of the visible behaviour. We can sometimes even be startled at our own behaviour. We can find ourselves wondering why we did what we did or said what we said. With the help of another we can sometimes begin to fathom what was really going on within us at the time, as we become more aware of the deeper issues that are significant for us.

In today's gospel reading, Jesus calls on us to look beyond the level of our behaviour to the deeper level of our emotions and our motivations. He calls for a virtue that goes deeper than that of the scribes and Pharisees, a way of life that has deep roots in good soil. Jesus takes two forms of behaviour that are clearly in conflict with the Ten Commandments, murder and adultery. He then goes to the deeper roots of such behaviour, anger in the case of murder and lust in the case of adultery. He thereby declares that what is of paramount importance is our depths, our inner life, which is known only to ourselves and is not readily visible to others. The first reading suggests, however, that our inner life is also known to God, 'For vast is the wisdom of the Lord; he is almighty and all-seeing.'

Paul, in today's second reading, makes reference to the inner life, the hidden depths, of God. This is the 'hidden wisdom of God' that 'no eye has seen and no ear has heard; things beyond the human mind'. These hidden depths of God can only be revealed to us, according to Paul, 'through the Spirit' who reaches 'even the depths of God'. If the Holy Spirit can reveal the depths of God to us, the same Holy Spirit can reveal our own hidden depths to us. Such revelation can sometimes be difficult for us to receive and accept. We can be slow to face up to what it is that sometimes drives how we behave and how we relate to others. Yet, in today's gospel reading, Jesus invites us to explore our depths, to face the truth of whatever resides within our hearts. Facing our own inner truth is, ultimately, liberating. As Jesus states in John's gospel, 'You will know the truth, and the truth will make you free.' When we look into our depths, it will certainly not be all bad. Something of what Paul calls 'the depths of God' reside within our own depths. As the first reading reminds us, 'to behave faithfully' is within our power. As Christians, we can say this with even greater conviction than the author of the book of Ecclesiasticus because, through baptism, Christ dwells deep within us. The deeper we enter into ourselves, the closer we come to the Lord. To act out of what is deepest in us is to act out of the Lord.

We know from experience that, at times, we act out of places within ourselves that have not been fully penetrated by the Lord's presence. We are aware of the anger and the lust within us that the Lord refers to in the gospel reading and that can lead us to behave in ways that are not in keeping with our baptismal identity. In the imagery of today's first reading, we sometimes put out our hand towards the fire rather than the water; we grasp death rather than life. Paul in his letters refers to this as acting 'according to the flesh' rather than 'according to the Spirit'. We know that there are areas within our hidden depths that have not been fully redeemed. We can easily make our own the prayer of Psalm 51: 'Create in me a clean heart, O God, and put a new and right spirit within me.' We need to keep on praying in that vein, asking the Lord to renew our depths. Yet, there will also be practical things we ourselves can do to help the Lord to create renewed depths within us. In today's gospel reading, Jesus suggests that radical action can sometimes be called for: 'If your right eye should cause you to sin, tear it our and throw it away … if your right hand should cause you to sin, cut it off and throw it away.' Jesus often spoke in exaggerated terms for effect. Today we might ask ourselves what concrete actions we need to take to make space for the Lord to renew our depths.

Seventh Sunday in Ordinary Time

The terminology of today's gospel reading has made its way into our day to day speech. We often speak of someone turning the other cheek or going the extra mile. Our initial reaction to hearing today's gospel might be to think that it is not very practical. Yes, it is a wonderful ideal, but it is impossible to achieve. It is good to have such a noble text among our scriptures, but we can hardly be expected to take it too seriously. Surely, this is a case of Jesus overstating something for effect.

Yet, that kind of reaction may point more to our own unease with this challenging text than to any problem with the message itself. At the beginning of the Sermon on the Mount, Jesus called for a virtue that goes deeper than that of the scribes and Pharisees, a way of life that was a step beyond what the Jewish Law required. Today's gospel reading is the fullest statement of this deeper virtue that Jesus calls for. The Old Testament stipulation of 'an eye for eye and tooth for tooth' was an enlightened effort at the time to put some limits on the extent to which people could retaliate for some injury inflicted on them. The tendency towards disproportionate retaliation had become the norm, several eyes for one eye and several teeth for one tooth. The teaching of Jesus goes beyond this attempt to limit retaliation by calling for no retaliation at all. There is to be no room for vengeance on a personal level among Jesus' followers.

Jesus calls on his followers not only not to take vengeance on the enemy, those who do them harm, but to go further and to love the enemy. He thereby calls for a love that is comprehensively inclusive. As one commentator on this passage puts it, 'Who else is left to love, after one has loved the enemy?' The love Jesus speaks of is not just a feeling but finds expression in active service. We might think of the parable of the good Samaritan, in which the Samaritan renders loving service to the injured Jew, who would have been regarded by the Samaritan as an enemy. Such a love of the enemy will also find expression in prayer for the enemy, as when Jesus asked his Father to forgive those who were responsible for his crucifixion. The human tendency is to restrict the scope of our service of others and of our prayer for others. We tend to focus our love on those we find attractive, those for whom we have strong feelings of warmth and affection. This is natural, but in the language of the gospel reading, it is not exceptional.

Jesus calls on us to stretch beyond those our love would naturally embrace. This is one of the gospel texts that does indeed stretch us. Human wisdom might argue against allowing ourselves to be stretched in this way. In loving the enemy, are we not leaving ourselves open to being taken advantage of? Is it not the case that charity begins at home, among those who are nearest and dearest to us? Yet, as Paul reminds us in today's second reading, 'the wisdom of this world is foolishness to God' and 'God is not convinced by the arguments of the wise.' The wisdom of God is revealed in the life, death and resurrection of Christ. It is the wisdom of God that Jesus, as the one who embodies that wisdom, presents in today's gospel reading. There is a gap between God's wisdom and what passes for human wisdom; God's ways are not our ways and God's thoughts are not our thoughts. In today's gospel reading, Jesus is calling on his disciples to move in the direction of God's ways, to reflect, to some degree, by our way of relating to others, the God who in love causes the sun to rise on bad people as well as good, and the rain to fall on honest and dishonest alike.

If we consider this to be beyond us, we have the assurance of Paul in today's second reading that we, the Lord's followers, are God's temple and that God's Spirit is living among us. The way of life that Jesus calls us towards is only possible in the power of the Spirit that lives among us and within us. Jesus calls for a way of relating that is truly of God and he also offers us the Spirit of God to enable us to respond to that call. The perfection or completeness that the gospel calls for is not primarily the fruit of our own efforts but, rather, the fruit of the Spirit. As Paul reminds the believers in Thessalonica, 'The one who calls you is faithful and he will accomplish this.'

Eighth Sunday in Ordinary Time

In the world of business and commerce the setting of priorities is considered essential. Companies set themselves goals and targets at the beginning of the year and assess whether they have reached them at the end of the year. Likewise, in the world of education, teachers have certain aims and objectives as they begin to teach a certain subject or a certain programme. Goals and targets, aims and objectives, keep people focused and help channel energies in a certain direction. In our own personal lives, as distinct from our professional lives, we also have certain priorities for ourselves that we try to aim towards. Having priorities keeps not only our energies focused but our anxieties focused as well, so that we worry about what is worth worrying about rather than about what is not.

In today's gospel reading, Jesus reveals his own priorities to his disciples: 'Set your hearts on (God's) kingdom first, and on his righteousness.' Jesus lived and died to advance the coming of God's kingdom; his focus was God's righteousness, the doing of God's will, by means of which God's kingdom would come. The priority of Jesus' life was, 'not my will, but yours be done'. He gave himself to the doing of God's will. That was his major preoccupation, his primary anxiety. In the striving for the coming of God's kingdom, in the struggle to do God's will, Jesus was prepared to let go of many material comforts and, indeed, to let go of life itself. His striving for God's kingdom meant that he would have nowhere to lay his head; it also meant that he would be rejected by the powerful and, finally, crucified.

Jesus not only gave himself to the doing of God's will but also to making God's will known so that others would do it. He wanted his disciples to have the same priorities that he had, to set their hearts on God's kingdom first, and on God's righteousness, the way of life that is in accordance with God's will. This is to be their fundamental goal in life, shaping and determining all their other goals and targets, all their aims and objectives. If they are to worry, this is what they are to worry about. Jesus wants his disciples to have the same preoccupation as he has. Yet he speaks in today's gospel reading out of an awareness that we are often anxious and troubled about what is not really of any ultimate importance. This was the fretful anxiety that characterised Martha in Luke's gospel, and whom Jesus addresses as 'worried and distracted by many things' while missing out on the 'one thing' that mattered, namely, attending to Jesus' word so as to know and do God's will. We know from our own experience that we can become very preoccupied about matters that, in reality, are not that important. The preoccupation with food and dress that Jesus refers to in today's gospel reading has something of a contemporary ring to it. A lot of energy and expense can be invested in looking well.

Today's gospel invites us to ask ourselves, 'What am I investing myself in?' 'What is important to me?' 'What do I have my heart set on?' 'What do I get anxious about?' In John's gospel, Jesus says of himself: 'My food is to do the will of him who sent me and to complete his work.' Jesus lived his life out of his deepest hungers and thirsts, rather than out of surface hungers and thirsts. In today's gospel reading, he calls on us to do the same. It is the pagans, he says, who live out of surface hungers and thirsts, and who set their hearts on what does not ultimately satisfy. In giving his disciples the Lord's prayer, Jesus was giving them a set of priorities that is worthy of the focus of all their hearts, souls, minds and strength: the hallowing of God's name; the coming of God's kingdom; the doing of God's will; enough bread for the day; forgiveness for our sins and our readiness to forgive others; God's help when we are put to the test. Here is a prayer that can help to keep us focused in the way that the Lord wants us to be focused.

If today's readings put before us priorities that belong to disciples of Jesus, they also remind us that we ourselves are the Lord's priority. According to today's first reading, God is even more committed to us that a mother is to her child. The gospel reading assures us that we are worth much more in the Lord's eyes than the birds in the sky that are the object of the Lord's care. In making us his priority, the Lord thereby empowers us to make him our priority.

Ninth Sunday in Ordinary Time

It is striking that a great deal of work can go on in a building site over a long period of time without much appearing above ground. Deep holes are dug by great machines; cement is poured into trenches; metal rods are inserted where they are needed. Once all this preparatory work is completed, the actual visible part of the building can emerge quite quickly. The most important part of a building is its foundations. If they are not right, the building itself will never be right. It makes sense to give careful consideration and attentive labour to the foundations, to what is below ground. It is often the case in life that what cannot be seen is more important than what can be seen.

In today's gospel reading, Jesus speaks a parable about two houses. To the external observer both houses probably would have looked very similar. There would have been no visible difference between the two buildings. The real difference between the houses lay in what was not visible to the naked eye, the foundations on which the houses were built. It was only the brute force of the storm that revealed the significant differences between the two houses that looked the same. Appearances can be deceptive; all is not always as it appears to be. What looks good to the outside observer, in reality may be fatally flawed.

Jesus was aware that what was true of houses could be equally true of people, including those who claimed to be his disciples. Some disciples looked very impressive to the outside observer; they were renowned for spectacular healings; they publicly addressed Jesus in all the right ways, 'Lord, Lord'; they often spoke powerful words in Jesus' name. They would, no doubt, have had a very devoted following. Yet, Jesus declares that such disciples can be strangers to him; at the end of the day, he may not recognise anything of himself in them. What was above ground looked impressive, even somewhat spectacular, but what was below ground left a lot to be desired. Such disciples were not well rooted or grounded.

What Jesus looks for in his followers is not the spectacular or the unusual, but rather what he terms 'doing the will of my Father in heaven'. These are the disciples whose lives are built on rock and with whom Jesus immediately identifies. They have something of that rock-like quality that today's responsorial psalm associates with the Father of Jesus, 'you are my rock, my stronghold'. What does 'doing the will of my Father in heaven' amount to? In a sense, the whole of Jesus' Sermon on the Mount spells out what it means in practice to do God's will. It entails living forgivingly, chastely, faithfully, truthfully, non-violently and, even, loving one's enemies. The remainder of Matthew's gospel also explores what it means to do God's will. In the language of the last judgement scene, with which Matthew concludes his account of the public ministry of Jesus, doing God's will entails giving food to the hungry and drink to the thirsty, welcoming the stranger and clothing the naked, visiting the sick and those in prison. This puts the real core of what it means to be a follower of Jesus in the realm of everyday life. Not mystical experiences or charismatic gifts, or even correct confessions of faith, but practical deeds of love are what identify someone as a disciple of Jesus. Much of this practical love in action may go unnoticed; it will generally not make any headlines. Like the foundations of a house, it will often be invisible to most observers. Yet, such actions are visible to the Lord and instantly recognisable by him as a reflection of his own life and ministry.

In today's second reading, Paul declares that a person is justified, or acceptable to God, on the basis of faith rather than on the basis of doing the works of the Jewish Law. Today's gospel reading reminds us that, for Jesus, faith always finds expression in action. As Jesus stated at the beginning of the Sermon on the Mount, the light of our faith shines before others when it finds expression in doing good works. As Paul declares in his letter to the Galatians: 'The only thing that counts is faith working through love.' However, the doing of faith requires a prior listening. It is those who listen to the words of Jesus and then act on them who are truly wise. We need to embody both the attitude of Mary, the sister of Martha, who sat at the Lord's feet and listened to him speaking, and the attitude of the Samaritan who busied himself with doing what was needed to bring back to life the broken Jew whom he stumbled upon on the road.

Tenth Sunday in Ordinary Time

A picture or a painting can often communicate more powerfully than the spoken or written word. I have a print in my living room of a painting of the call of Matthew by the Italian artist Caravaggio. In the painting Matthew is sitting at a table in a house with a number of other people. Jesus stands to one side having just come into the room. He looks at Matthew and points very deliberately towards him; Matthew looks at Jesus and points to himself. It is as if Matthew is saying to Jesus, 'Who, me?' He was after all a tax collector, in the pay of the occupying Roman power, and such people were universally despised. They were also considered 'sinners' by those who thought of themselves as 'religious'. Caravaggio captures the amazement on the part of Matthew that someone as good as Jesus would call on someone as bad as himself.

Jesus saw something in Matthew that nobody else saw, and that not even Matthew saw in himself. When other people looked at Matthew, they saw a sinner. When Jesus looked at him, he saw a saint. The gospels suggest that Jesus had that ability to see what people could become. Jesus struggled at times to get people to see in themselves what he could see in them. Jesus believed in people when others did not, and when perhaps they had even stopped believing in themselves. He first showed that he believed in them before calling on them to believe in him.

There are many differences between us as we gather in church here today, but one thing we all have in common is that we are sinners. We have all fallen short of what the Lord wants for us. In the process we may have done damage to ourselves and to others. Today's gospel reading assures us that when the Lord looks on us, he does not only see the wrong we have done and the good we have failed to do. He also sees the good we have done, and the good we can do and have yet to do. His way of looking at us, like his way of looking at Matthew, is generous and merciful. The Lord is not in the business of locking us into our past; he is much more about calling us beyond where we have been and where we are, and helping us to get to where he is calling us. He points to us not in an accusing way but, rather, in an inviting way.

This is not only how the Lord relates to us, but also how he wants us to relate to each other. He says to us what he says to the Pharisees in today's gospel reading: 'What I want is mercy and not sacrifice.' The Pharisees had written off people like Matthew, and saw no point in associating with his likes. There can be something of the Pharisees in all of us. We can be tempted to define people by the wrong they have done, rather than by the good they are capable of doing and have yet to do. Our way of seeing someone can be very limited. When our way of seeing is so limited, we end up expecting little from people and we fail to call them forth. Because Jesus' way of seeing people was merciful and generous, he called them forth in ways that set them on the path to becoming what God intended them to become. Like him, we need to be open to seeing more than what is immediately obvious.

In the gospel reading, Jesus not only calls Matthew, who subsequently becomes one of the twelve, but he went on to share table with Matthew and with other tax collectors and sinners. That scene of Jesus sharing table points ahead to the last time Jesus would share table with his disciples at the Last Supper, which was the first Eucharist. Every Eucharist has something of the character of the table sharing we read about in today's gospel. It is a table sharing between Jesus and sinners. At every Eucharist we gather as people who have failed in various ways. That is why we begin every Mass by calling to mind our sins. At every Eucharist we experience what Matthew and the others experienced at table with Jesus. We experience someone who looks mercifully upon us, who points towards us more in an inviting than in an accusing way. At every Eucharist we also hear those words addressed to us that Matthew and the others heard at table: 'What I want is mercy, not sacrifice.' The Lord sends us out from the Eucharist with the call to relate to each other in the same merciful and generous way that he has related to us.

Eleventh Sunday in Ordinary Time

In many parts of the western world the numbers to be ordained priest will be small for the foreseeable future, and the numbers leaving fulltime active ministry due to retirement and other reasons will continue to grow.

That is the context in which we are asked to reflect on the words of Jesus in today's gospel reading: 'The harvest is great but the labourers are few, so ask the Lord of the harvest to send labourers into his harvest.' We have tended to hear those words of Jesus as primarily an invitation to pray for more vocations to the priesthood and religious life. However, we have come to a greater appreciation in more recent times that when the Lord asks us to pray for 'labourers', we need to think of a much broader group than just the ordained and the religiously professed. The Lord sent all kinds of labourers into his harvest in the course of his ministry. As well as the twelve apostles mentioned in today's gospel reading, he also sent out a group of seventy two, as well as people like the Samaritan woman, Mary Magdalene, and many others. The harvest was great, and all kinds of labourers were needed. Some of these labourers had spent a lot of time with Jesus, like the twelve apostles. Others had spent relatively little time in his company before beginning to labour in his harvest, like the Samaritan woman.

Jesus' understanding of who qualifies to be a labourer in the Lord's harvest is as broad today as it was when he ministered in Galilee. It may be that the reason why so few people are presenting themselves as candidates for the ordained priesthood and the religious life today, at least in the more developed world, is because the Lord is not calling as many people to the priesthood or religious life today as he did in the past. The Lord may be reminding us of something very obvious – something that has always been the church's teaching – namely, that the sacrament of baptism is more important than the sacrament of ordination, and that in virtue of our baptism we are all called to be labourers in the Lord's harvest. When Jesus asks us to pray the Lord of the harvest to send labourers into his harvest, he is asking us to pray that all the baptised will take seriously their own baptismal calling to share in the Lord's mission in the world. In the first reading today, the Lord informs Moses that he considers the whole people to be a kingdom of priests and a consecrated nation. What was true of the people of Israel is even truer of the members of the church.

There have always been movements in the church that enabled lay men and women to become labourers in the Lord's harvest. There is much happening in the church today that also reflects Jesus' broad understanding of who are to be regarded as labourers in his harvest. The emergence of parish pastoral councils is one example of a structure at parish level that makes possible a more collaborative style of pastoral leadership involving both priests and laity. One of the tasks of a parish pastoral council is to create opportunities for people in a parish to use their gifts and their experience in the service of the wider parish community. In the gospel reading, Jesus calls on the twelve to go only to the lost sheep of the house of Israel. It is only later that he will send them out to make disciples of all the nations. They must first work locally before they are to go further afield. The local expression of the Lord's harvest is where most of us will be called to labour. We need to build up the local church before it can become truly missionary. For parents, that local harvest is first of all the home, what has been called the domestic church. The domestic church needs parental shepherds today more than ever before.

We are all called to be labourers in the Lord's harvest because we have all received something precious. As Jesus says in today's gospel reading: 'You received without charge, give without charge.' What we have received is well expressed for us by Paul in today's second reading: 'What proves that God loves us is that Christ died for us while we were still sinners.' Having been reconciled to God by the death of his Son, Paul assures us that we will be saved by the life of his Son. In the person of his Son, God has already graced us abundantly and will grace us further. In response to being graced in this way, we are all called to become labourers in the Lord's harvest, giving as we have received.

Twelfth Sunday in Ordinary Time

In all our lives there are areas that are quite public and other areas that are very private. We are happy to talk about some things in the public forum, but careful to talk about other matters only in the privacy of our home, or perhaps not at all. The line between the private and the public can vary between one person and another. Issues that some people might consider to be of legitimate public interest might be regarded by others as belonging exclusively in the private domain. Whereas we might consider some people too closed, keeping private what could easily be shared with others, we might think of others as too open, sharing too easily what would better be kept private.

In today's gospel reading, Jesus says: 'What I say to you in the dark, tell in the daylight; what you hear in whispers, proclaim from the house-tops.' It is clear from the context that what Jesus wants people to tell in the daylight, to proclaim from the housetops, is the gospel, the good news that Jesus himself preached and lived. Jesus wants his disciples to declare themselves for him publicly, to acknowledge him openly.

When we look at the private areas and the public areas of our lives, where does our faith belong? Do we see it as belonging more to the private area or to the public area? In more recent decades, there has been a tendency for believers to retreat somewhat from the public domain. Many of us have become more circumspect about witnessing to our faith. We are less likely to publicly declare our allegiance to Christ. We sense that the environment has become more hostile to the gospel, and in that we are probably right. The recent exposure of scandals in the church has been one factor in all of this. There is a danger that we will have a collective loss of nerve when it comes to the gospel and to the church, through and in which, for all its faults, we receive and hear the gospel.

This Sunday's readings have something important to say to us in that context. Three times in the course of the gospel reading, Jesus calls on his disciples not to be afraid. The fear he is talking about is the fear of witnessing publicly to the values he proclaimed by his life, death and resurrection. We all have a whole variety of legitimate fears. Parents will be fearful of their children getting into trouble; we are all fearful of a nuclear arms race, of the consequences of growing inequality both at home and on a more global scale. There are many things about which we need a healthy fear. However, Jesus strongly indicates in today's gospel reading that one thing we should not be fearful of is bearing public witness to himself and his gospel.

In saying to his disciple, 'Do not be afraid', Jesus was not trying to minimise the opposition they would encounter when they began to proclaim the gospel by their lives. He is not saying to them or to us, 'do not be afraid because there is nothing to fear'. There is a set of values embodied in the gospel, in our faith, that are very challenging and will be experienced as threatening by some, perhaps even by ourselves from time to time. There can often be a risk in taking a public stand for gospel values, such as the respect for life at all its stages, justice for all, the fundamental equality of all men and women under God, the priority of forgiveness over revenge, of serving over acquiring. Jesus was saying, 'Do not be afraid because when you courageously bear witness to me and my gospel, God will be watching over you', or, in the words of Jeremiah in today's first reading, 'The Lord is at my side.' The gospel reading is assuring us that the Father cares deeply for those disciples who have the courage to live publicly their faith in Jesus and his gospel.

St Paul in one of his letters speaks about carrying a treasure in earthen jars. He was referring to the treasure of the gospel, and he understood himself to be the earthen jar. We are all carrying a treasure in earthen jars. The fact that we show ourselves to be all too earthen from time to time does not make what we carry any the less of a treasure. In today's gospel reading Jesus assures his disciples of their worth: 'You are worth more than hundreds of sparrows.' Who we are as Christians and the values that we stand for are of inestimable worth. If we really appreciated that worth, it would go a long way towards making us less fearful about the public living of our faith.

Thirteenth Sunday in Ordinary Time

I recently came across a story from the Jewish tradition that appealed to me. It tells of a Jewish rabbi who used to disappear into the forest on the evening of every Sabbath. His congregation presumed that he was going into the forest to commune with God in prayer. One Sabbath the congregation chose one of their members to follow the rabbi into the forest. They were hoping that in this way they might gain some insight into the rabbi's prayer. The member of the congregation set out after the rabbi, keeping a discreet distance. Deeper and deeper into the woods the rabbi went until he came to the cottage of an old woman who was very badly crippled. Once there, the rabbi cooked for her, carried her firewood and swept the house. Then when all the chores were done, he returned immediately to his little house next to the synagogue and began his prayers. When the member of the congregation who had followed the rabbi returned to the village, the people asked him: 'Well, did our rabbi go up to heaven, as we thought he would?' After some pause for thought, the one who had followed the rabbi replied, 'Oh no. He went much higher than that.'

In the gospel reading today Jesus says that anyone who loses his life for his sake will find it. Jesus states the paradox that we find ourselves by giving ourselves away. The manner in which we give ourselves away may be hidden to others, as in the case of the rabbi in the story. In the gospel reading Jesus declares that if anyone gives so much as a cup of cold water to one of the little ones among his disciples, they will most certainly not loose their reward. Giving a cup of cold water to someone who needs it is not going to make headlines. Most likely, only the giver and the receiver will be aware of it. Yet, Jesus holds up this small act as having eternal consequences. The giving of a cup of cold water can stand for any number of small acts of kindness which give life to others in some way.

In the gospel reading Jesus is trying to teach us the value of what we might be inclined to dismiss as of very little significance. In all sorts of ways throughout this parish, this city, people are giving the equivalent of a cup of cold water to those who need it. Parents are doing it for their children every day of the week, especially in those times when children fall ill. Neighbours are doing as much for each other, young people for those who have less vitality and energy than themselves. The kind of hospitality shown by the woman to Elisha is being replicated every day in all kinds of ways among us.

We can all think of people who have shown us hospitality over the years. Such hospitality may have taken a whole variety of forms, apart from food at a table or a bed for the night. We appreciate those who make us feel at home when we move into some new situation, whether it is a new location or a new job or a new responsibility. We value those who are hospitable towards us when we need a listening ear. Such welcoming responses are all expressions of that giving of the cup of cold water that Jesus speaks about in today's gospel reading. Jesus who came not to be served but to serve was himself very appreciative of the cup of cold water from others. In the heat of a noon sun he asked the Samaritan woman for a drink; he welcomed the hospitality of people like Mary and Martha; he found momentary relief when Simon of Cyrene helped him carry his cross.

Jesus indicates in today's gospel reading that when hospitality is shown to others, there is more going on than we might realise at the time. He states: 'Anyone who welcomes you welcomes me; and those who welcome me welcome the one who sent me.' The way we relate to each other is an expression of how we are relating to Jesus and the Father, whether we are aware of that or not. In that sense, life is not divided into a secular area and a sacred area, the secular area being where we live, work and play, and the sacred where we pray and worship. The secular is shot through with the sacred. In our dealings with human flesh we are dealing with the divine. We stand on holy ground all the time, and the burning bush is everywhere. The giving of the cup of cold water is more significant than we realise – and so too is the failure to give it.

Fourteenth Sunday in Ordinary Time

Sometimes when things are going against us, it can be difficult to be positive about anything. After several negative experiences we can be tempted to see everything with a jaundiced eye. Those experiences that leave us feeling angry, sad and hurt can affect our ability to notice all that we still have reason to be grateful for. You come across people occasionally who have very little good to say about anyone or anything. Perhaps they have had deeply negative experiences in life and this has left them with a negative outlook on everything.

Just before the passage that we find in this morning's gospel reading, Jesus was complaining about the people of his generation. They found fault with John the Baptist because he lived too austere a lifestyle, and they found fault with Jesus because he lived too gregarious a lifestyle. It seems that Jesus had very good reason to be negative about many of his contemporaries. Yet, the negative experiences that he had did not blind him to all the good that was happening around him and for which he could be grateful. Having complained about his contemporaries, he then went on to give thanks and praise to God for all those who were responding to what God was doing in and through him. That is what we find Jesus doing in today's gospel reading. Many of those who would have been considered the least significant in the land were seeing what the wise and intelligent were failing to see. Jesus could say to this group, 'Come to me', in the knowledge that they would respond.

Jesus had that capacity to recognise the signs of life in what seemed like a desert. He was attuned to the mysterious ways in which God was working, even when what was more obvious were the ways that people were turning away from God. Even after many negative experiences of failure and rejection, he knew that that there were many reasons why God should be praised and thanked. Unlike Jesus, we may be inclined to bless and praise God only when we feel that all is going well. We can be slow to see the workings of God in situations that fall short of our hopes and expectations. Yet, God is always at work, even in the most distressing experiences and in the most unpromising of situations. If we can step back from what is happening and look carefully we might begin to notice that the Lord is there. He is present in those who care for us and journey with us through the valley of darkness, in the small signs which indicate that our good efforts are bearing some fruit.

What is true of our personal lives is also true of the life of our church. Some of us looking at the church today may be tempted to become very negative. There can appear to be a great deal of failure and loss in our church today. If that becomes our only focus, we may fail to notice the new ways that God is working among the followers of his Son, the signs of new life that are there in the church, if we only look deeply enough.

The readings today suggest that it is easy to miss the many ways that the Lord is moving among us. The prophet Zechariah in the first reading announced the arrival of a king who would come humble and riding on a donkey. People of that culture did not expect kings to ride on donkeys but on war horses. If they saw someone coming towards them on a donkey, they would never suspect that he was a king. Zechariah was suggesting to the people that God's messenger will come to them in a very ordinary and, to many, a very unpromising way. As a result they might fail to notice him when he is among them.

It is certainly hard to image anything less promising than a crucified man, and yet, in that man God was reaching out to humanity in love. The evangelists suggest that the Roman centurion was one of very few to recognise the powerful presence of God in this most bleak of moments. Indeed, Luke tells us that when the centurion saw what had taken place he praised God.

In today's gospel reading, Jesus assures us that he is especially near to us when we are labouring under the weight of some heavy burden. In those dark times when we might be tempted to think that the Lord has abandoned us, he is, in reality, calling out to us to come to him. Even in such times, there is good reason to praise and thank God. We pray for the eyes to see the signs of the Lord's presence in our own painful moments.

Fifteenth Sunday in Ordinary Time

Most of us value success. When we apply ourselves to some task and the results are good, we feel satisfied. When our successful efforts are recognised by others, it is all the better. There can be a lot of pressure on people today to succeed. Resources of various kinds are made available to people to help them succeed in the task they have set themselves. In a culture that values success, failure can be hard to cope with, whether it is failure in school or at work or in a relationship. Not measuring up to our own expectations or those of others can leave people feeling demoralised, or even depressed.

In the gospel reading, Jesus tells a short story in which both failure and success feature. The sower who goes out to sow the seed meets with both. Much of what he scatters on the ground is wasted. There are a whole variety of obstacles impeding his work, the birds, the rocks, the thorns. He can do very little about these obstacles. They are part of his world. He knows he has to make allowances for them, but they don't stop him casting the seed. He is confident that in spite of all these obstacles and the inevitable failure that results, some of the seed will take root and mature, and that, at the end of the day, there will be a harvest to bring in.

When Jesus originally told this story, he was talking about himself and his work. He was the sower who scattered the seed of God's word. Much of what he said and did met with little or no response from people. What he had to say very often fell on deaf ears; what he did was often misunderstood. The people he had chosen to be his closest followers often showed themselves to be unresponsive pupils. Yet, Jesus was saying in this story, that, in spite of all these obstacles and failures, he would continue with the work that God had given him to do. He would keep sowing in spite of unfavourable odds, because he knew that at the end of the day, the harvest would be great. God's word would not return to him empty.

In telling that parable, Jesus was not only speaking about himself and his life, he was also giving us a way of looking at our own lives. The parable suggests that there are times in life when we need to keep sowing even in the face of unfavourable odds. This is not to suggest that we are called to keep hitting our head off a stone wall indefinitely. There are situations in which the prudent thing to do is to throw in the towel. There were towns that Jesus simply had to walk away from because no one wanted him there. Yet, there are times when we have to keep on doing whatever good we can, even when it appears that the obstacles seem insurmountable. When we are engaged in something worthwhile, and things are going against us, we could probably find all kinds of reasons why we should pull back or give up. Various versions of the birds of the air and of the rocky and thorny soil can threaten to wear us down. In such situations the Lord may be calling us to be faithful to the good work we are doing. It was mother Teresa of Calcutta who said that the Lord does not ask us to be successful but to be faithful. When we look around us we can see examples of that kind of fidelity in the face of huge odds. I think of those who continue to invest in someone even though the return is minimal, or those who keep working away at some worthwhile cause even when they seem to be getting nowhere.

This kind of human persistence is an image of how the Lord relates to each of us. The parable suggests that the Lord gives the most unlikely places the opportunity to receive his word and respond to it. The human tendency is to assess the likely return before making an investment. Today's parable indicates that the Lord is not nearly as calculating as we often are. He casts his word, his Spirit, liberally, without discrimination. The unpromising soil is treated as generously as the good soil. This is in keeping with what Jesus said of God a little earlier in Matthew's gospel, remarking that God makes his sun rise on the evil and the good, and sends rain on the righteous and unrighteous. This is not meant to make us complacent. But it is reassuring to know that God is wasteful and persistent in our regard; it encourages us to keep on responding to him, even after failure.

Sixteenth Sunday in Ordinary Time

Most of us who do a bit of gardening expect to have a weed-free garden. We see weeds as as something to be got rid of. Some of us may have discovered that our zeal to get rid of weeds can have unfortunate consequences. In my ignorance I once sprayed a lawn that had weeds among the grass with a weed killer. I succeeded only in killing off the grass; the weeds seemed to have got a new lease of life. In going after weeds, we can do a certain amount of unintended collateral damage.

We can easily identify with the servants in the gospel reading who were poised to pull up the weeds that an enemy had sown in the wheat field of their master. However, the owner of the field was a more patient man. He recognised that at the early stages of growth weeds can look very like wheat and that it can be very difficult to distinguish between the two. In going after the weeds, the wheat would suffer too. He saw that it would be better to wait until both the weed and the wheat got much bigger and were ready for harvest. Then it would be possible to distinguish one from the other and to separate them accordingly. The owner knew that there was a time to leave well enough alone and there was a time to act. The time when the servants wanted to act was really the time to leave well enough alone. The servants had zeal but not much insight, and zeal without insight can be very dangerous.

The parable suggests that doing nothing can sometimes be better than doing something. Jesus may have been alerting his followers to the dangers of a certain kind of well-intentioned zeal that demanded immediate action, when patient inactivity would actually be the better option. When Jesus was once refused entry into a Samaritan village, his disciples asked him if he wanted them to call on God to rain down fire from heaven and destroy the village. No doubt the disciples considered that Samaritan village to be the equivalent of the weeds in the wheat field of today's parable. The evangelist tells us that Jesus rebuked his disciples and went on to another village. History, even recent history, is full of the tragic consequences of the kind of attitude displayed by those disciples. It is the attitude that says that the world would be a better place without such and such a person or without such and such a group, and, therefore, the right thing to do, the godly thing to do, is to take zealous action to remove such people or such groups from the world. Weed them out! The zeal of the weed killer can be a frightening thing.

Jesus in the parable was warning us against a premature separation of the wheat from the weed, of the good from the bad. He was saying that this kind of separation is really God's work, not our work, and that it will happen at the end of time rather than in the course of time. Just as the servants in the parable would not have been able to distinguish the wheat from the weeds if they had been let loose, we do not always have the necessary insight to distinguish who is good and who is evil. How often in our own personal lives have we judged someone harshly only to discover in time that we were very wide of the mark. Unfortunately, the church itself has not always heeded the warning of Jesus about the dangers of premature separation. It could be argued that the inquisition was not in the spirit of the parable that Jesus speaks in today's gospel reading. Too great a zeal to purify the wheat field risks doing more harm than good.

A weed-free garden may be highly desirable, but the gospel today suggests that we may have to learn to live with weeds. We need to be patient with imperfection in ourselves and in others. As we know only too well, life is not tidy. It is not like a well manicured garden, in which order and harmony prevail. Our own personal lives are not like the garden displays that win prizes at the Chelsea flower show. Each of us is a mixture of wheat and weed; we are each tainted by sin and yet touched by grace. Our calling is to grow in grace before God and others, as Jesus did. We look to him to help us to keep on turning from sin and growing in grace. St Paul assures us in today's second reading that the Spirit helps us in our weakness. With the Spirit's help we can grow more and more into the person of Christ.

Seventeenth Sunday in Ordinary Time

You sometimes hear it said that he or she is very ambitious. As a rule, such an observation is not meant as a complement. Yet, ambition in itself is neither negative nor positive. What determines whether ambition is praiseworthy or blameworthy is the object of our ambition. Today's first reading presents us with an expression of praiseworthy ambition. In response to the Lord's invitation, 'Ask what you would like me to give you', Solomon replied, 'Give your servant a heart to understand how to discern between good and evil.' Solomon's desire to have the wisdom he would need to govern God's people justly was an acceptable ambition in the Lord's eyes.

The Lord's invitation to Solomon, 'Ask what you would like me to give you', finds an echo in the question that Jesus would ask of his disciples, 'What is it you want me to do for you?' In responding to the invitation and the question, we reveal what it is we really value. The first two parables in today's gospel reading suggest that our primary ambition as followers of Jesus is to be 'the kingdom of heaven'. What is meant by 'the kingdom of heaven', or its equivalent, 'the kingdom of God'? The clue to its meaning is to be found in the opening petitions of the Lord's Prayer that Jesus gave to his disciples: 'Hallowed be your name, your kingdom come, your will be done.' To be ambitious for the kingdom of heaven is to be ambitious for the doing of God's will. The disciple of Jesus is someone who wants what God wants and who lives accordingly. It is Jesus who revealed God's will for our lives and who embodied that will in how he lived and died. To be ambitious for God's kingdom then is to be ambitious to become true images of God's Son, in the words of today's second reading. This is God's ambition for us; God always intended us to be true images of his Son. The gospel reading calls on us to make our ambition for ourselves and for others conform to God's ambition for us.

According to our second reading, God wants his Son to be the eldest of many brothers and sisters who bear the image of his Son. God wants a universal family, every one of whose members bears the image of God's own beloved Son. God's ambition is essentially communitarian in nature. To that extent our ambition for ourselves is inseparable from our ambition for others. We are to be ambitious for a community of people who are living images of God's Son, because this is what God wants. This is the treasure in the field, the pearl of great price. Such a community is what the Book of Revelation speaks of as the heavenly city, the new Jerusalem, which will emerge at the end of time when God has overcome all the powers of evil. Yet, it is God's ambition, and ours, that the shape of such a city would be visible among us now. That is why Jesus calls on us to pray, 'Your will be done on earth as in heaven.' Our earthly communities are to reflect the heavenly community of the end of time.

We can sometimes, to our amazement, stumble upon the kind of community that God wants, where God's will is done, like the poor farm labourer who unexpectedly came upon treasure hidden in the field where he was working. He was not looking for any treasure at the time; without searching, he found something of great worth. Like this farm labourer, we too can be surprised by joy as we unexpectedly discover an expression of God's kingdom in the here and now. Like the farm labourer, we may be moved by this joyful discovery to let go of our old ways of living so as to embrace this treasure that speaks to us of God who is Love.

The main character in the second parable Jesus speaks is not a poor farm labourer but a rich merchant who does not unexpectedly stumble upon a treasure he had not been looking for. Rather, he had invested a great deal of himself in searching for a pearl of great price. Eventually, his painstaking search paid off and he found what he was looking for. His reaction to the find was the same as that of the poor farm labourer. He sold everything he owned to buy it. Like the merchant, our own finding of the earthly expression of God's heavenly community can come at the end of a long search, in response to the Lord's promise, 'Seek and you will find.' However we come upon what is of true worth, the gospel reading calls on us to take all necessary steps to grasp it.

Eighteenth Sunday in Ordinary Time

Whenever we are given bad news, we often feel the need to be on our own for a while. We need time away from our normal routine so as to take in what has happened. If someone close to us dies, for example, we need time to think about that person, to reflect on the relationship we had with him or her and to talk through what we are feeling and thinking with one or two trusted companions.

According to today's gospel reading, when Jesus heard the news of the beheading of his cousin John the Baptist, he cut short his active ministry and withdrew by boat to a lonely place where he could be with some of his closest disciples. The death of John must have disturbed Jesus. He no doubt foresaw his own fate in what had happened to John. Quiet time alone with those who would not make demands on him was needed. Yet, the gospel reading tells us that, by the time Jesus went to this lonely place with his disciples, it had become a crowded place. The crowds had got there ahead of him. His plans for a quiet, restful time completely unravelled. It would have been understandable if Jesus had reacted to this unexpected situation with anger. Instead, the evangelist tells us that he reacted with compassion. He began to give of himself to those who had sought him out, healing their sick.

We have all had the experience of plans not working out. We like to be in control of our lives. We like to think that what we intend to happen will happen. We have expectations of ourselves, of others, of our relationships, of our work situation. We imagine a certain kind of future for ourselves, both in the short term and in the long term. We then discover that what transpires is not what we had bargained for. Life has a way of throwing up the unexpected, and the unexpected can at times be unwelcome and demanding. When things do not work out as we had planned, we can react in various ways. We can allow anger and self-pity to take us over, or we can give ourselves generously to the new situation, even though it is not what we had hoped for. When we give ourselves generously to the unexpected, something very worthwhile can result. When Jesus gave himself generously to the unexpected, a great multitude was fed in the wilderness.

It is clear from today's gospel reading that Jesus' disciples were less inclined to give themselves to the unexpected than Jesus himself was. When evening came, the disciples said to Jesus: 'Send the people away, and they can go to the villages to buy themselves some food.' It is as if they were suggesting, 'Let us make this crowded place a lonely place once more. Let us get back to what we had planned.' When Jesus suggested that they themselves give the crowd something to eat they protested, 'All we have is five loaves and two fish.' I think most of us could readily sympathise with the disciples. The unexpected can sometimes be very disconcerting. When we find ourselves in a situation that we had not bargained for, we can be tempted to panic. In our anxiety, we can feel that we won't be able to cope with this new and demanding situation. Our initial reaction can often be to start thinking of various exit strategies.

Yet, today's gospel reading suggests that getting ourselves out of some unexpected situation that appears to overwhelm us may not be the only or even the best option open to us. The resources the disciples had available seemed to be insignificant. But Jesus took those resources and worked with them in a way that went far beyond the expectations of the disciples. The few resources they had at their disposal turned out to be more than enough, when shared with the Lord. The gospel reading suggests that when the unexpected threatens to overwhelm us, we are not alone. The Lord is with us, and if we face the situation with him, we will accomplish far more that we might have expected initially. When our own resources seem slight in comparison to what we are facing into, the Lord can work powerfully through them if we bring them to him. The little we give can turn out to be more than enough.

St Paul in the second reading tells us that nothing can come between us and the love of Christ. There is no situation that separates us from the loving presence of the Lord. There is no traumatic event that we cannot face with the Lord at our side. In the words of Paul in another of his letters, 'I can do all things in him who gives me strength.'

Nineteenth Sunday in Ordinary Time

We all need to find ways to relax from time to time. Different people relax in different ways. One of the ways many people relax is by walking. Walking has its own rhythm, and it can take you out of other rhythms that can be experienced as stressful. Most people are not very adventurous walkers, preferring level ground that is firm under foot. Others prefer more of a challenge when they go walking. They head for the hills, and the higher and steeper the better.

In today's gospel reading, Peter goes one better than most in terms of being adventurous. He steps out of his boat and begins to walk towards Jesus across the water. Walking on water is not something any of us would attempt. Yet, at a more symbolic level, Peter's walking on water can be an image of our lives from time to time. There are times when we can feel that the ground on which we stand is not all that solid. We sometimes say, for example, 'I'm not sure of my ground' or 'I don't know where I stand', when we are perplexed or confused about something. You hear people saying that it was like 'walking on egg shells' to describe a difficult conversation or meeting that they had with someone. Others speak about feeling as if the rug was pulled from under them to describe some deeply hurtful experience. Most of the time, we try to avoid these kinds of experiences that leave us feeling vulnerable. We often feel the urge to seek out solid ground and stay there at all costs.

Yet, there are times when we may need to step off our solid ground onto something that appears less secure. In the gospel reading, Jesus called Peter to step out of the boat and to come towards him across the water. Surely it would have been safer for Peter to stay in the boat. Why would Peter want to step out of the relative safety of his boat and to walk towards Jesus, and why would Jesus encourage him to do so? Perhaps the evangelist is reminding us through this story that following Jesus, walking after him or towards him, will sometimes mean stepping out of our boat, the place where we feel relatively secure, and launching out into the deep. Paul is a very good example of that. He was very secure in his life as a Pharisee. In today's second reading, he speaks of his 'brothers of Israel' in very emotional tones. Yet, in response to the Lord's call, he left the security of the Pharisaic tradition, where he was completely at home, and he headed out into something that must have seemed much less secure.

Today's gospel reading invites us to reflect on the ways that the Lord may be calling us to take some new step in our relationship with him. When it comes to our relationship with the Lord, it can be tempting to stay put, to keep to what we know, to hold on to what is familiar to us. Yet, the Lord is always calling us to offer ourselves to him in new ways. The Lord's call to 'come' will take different forms for different people. It may be an invitation to grow in our understanding of our faith through reading, reflection and study, or to use our gifts in a new way within the parish community. It might take the form of a call to become more prayerful, more attuned to the gentle breeze of the Lord's voice, referred to in today's first reading, or a call to take some step to become reconciled with someone from whom we have been estranged for a long time.

When we respond to that call of the Lord, when we step out into a new domain, our experience can be a little like that of Peter. We might sense that we are now out of our depth; we can begin to feel that we are sinking. We wonder why we ever left the boat in the first place, why we did not stay put. Today's gospel reading, however, assures us that whenever we respond to the Lord's invitation to 'come', he will be there to support us. Even when we begin to doubt him, the Lord does not lose faith in us. He will hear us when we cry out to him, 'Lord save me', and he will reach out to hold us firm and prevent us from sinking. The one who calls us to journey towards him does not leave us to our own devices when we respond to his call. He journeys with us, and if we keep turning towards him, we too, like Peter and the disciples, will find ourselves exclaiming, 'Truly, you are the Son of God.'

Twentieth Sunday in Ordinary Time

We tend to admire people who 'stick to their guns', who have a conviction about something and hold to it, even when put under strong pressure to do otherwise. We have less sympathy with those who change their views to suit the situation, who express one view to one person and a very different view to another person. We rightly feel that such people are not to be trusted or relied upon.

Yet, sticking to our guns is not always the best course of action. We need strong convictions based on the values of the gospel, but we also need to be flexible enough to allow our convictions to be shaped in new ways. Sometimes we discover, in dialogue with others, that there are dimensions to some issue that had not occurred to us; sometimes our experience of life teaches us that the issue is more complex than our conviction initially allowed for. As people of faith, we need to be open to the likelihood that the Lord has always something more to teach us, that our strongly held views may not always fully correspond to the Lord's view.

In today's gospel reading Jesus solemnly announces to the pagan woman, 'I was sent only to the lost sheep of the house of Israel.' Jesus understood that the initial focus of his mission, and that of his disciples, was to be the renewal of the people of Israel, his own compatriots; only later, after his death and resurrection, would there be a mission to the pagans. What we find happening in today's gospel reading is that Jesus allows this important conviction of his to be reshaped by the persistent pleading of a pagan woman on behalf of her sick child. Jesus met her initial plea with silence; he met her second plea with a comment that can seem a bit shocking to us today: 'It is not fair to take the children's food and throw it to the house-dogs.' The 'children' were the people of Israel; the 'house-dogs' was a standard term that Jews used with reference to the pagans. The woman was not deterred either by Jesus' initial silence or by his subsequent comment. With a mixture of perseverance, humility and humour, she expressed a willingness to eat the crumbs that fell from the children's table, as the house dogs often do. Jesus recognised what he called her 'great faith' and, in spite of his initial reluctance, ministered to her and her daughter there and then.

Here was a woman who succeeded in reshaping Jesus' strongly held conviction about the primary focus of his mission. The gospel reading suggests that Jesus recognised that the Spirit of God was speaking to him through her passionate love for her daughter and her equally passionate faith in God's presence in Jesus. This woman, from a Jewish point of view, was a complete outsider. Yet, she became, in a sense, Jesus' teacher, and Jesus allowed himself to be taught by her.

The gospel reading suggests to us that, like Jesus, we too need to be open to the Spirit speaking to us through those we meet on our life's journey. In our conversations with people, we can discover that some of our deeply held convictions are being unexpectedly challenged. Unlike Jesus, we may not have the freedom to respond to this challenge there and then. However, when we walk away from such conversations and begin to think about what was said, we can find ourselves questioning what we had been very sure about. It can happen that such questioning can bring on something of a crisis for us. We might even find ourselves wondering if our faith is growing weaker. It may be, however, that God is simply purifying our faith. God may be trying to open us up to a new horizon that we had not been aware of. God may be showing us that there is more to God's purpose for our world and for our lives than we had realised.

Jesus' convictions were reshaped by someone who was very much an outsider, a woman in a man's world, a pagan in a Jewish world. In a similar way today, those from whom we think we have the least to learn can often have the most to teach us. A pagan woman's passionate concern for her ailing daughter showed Jesus that the gospel ministry to the pagans could not wait until after his death and resurrection. The passionate commitment to the healing of others that is often to be found among those who do not see themselves as part of the church can sometimes reveal for us the deepest meaning of the gospel. We pray today for the openness to recognise and respond to the movement of the Spirit, wherever it is to be found.

Twenty-First Sunday of the Year

Most of us have at least one set of keys. If you are like me, you will loose one or other set from time to time. We know that keys have the power to open and shut, and we do not like to think of that power falling into the hands of strangers. We are careful about who we give our keys to. We give them only to those we really trust.

The first reading and gospel reading today make reference to the giving of keys to people. In the first reading, the Lord gives the key of the house of David to Eliakim. This key gave him the authority to open and to shut the palace in Jerusalem where the king, David's successor, lived. In today's gospel reading, Jesus promises to give the keys of the kingdom of heaven to Peter. The keys of a royal palace are one thing; the keys of the kingdom of heaven are quite another. Of course, Jesus was not speaking literally. The kingdom of heaven is not a purely earthly kingdom; there are no keys to it in the sense in which we all have house keys. However, the language of giving keys suggests that Jesus is investing Peter with significant authority – authority not in the sense of power, but in the sense of responsibility and service. It is extraordinary that the Christ, the Son of the living God, should give such responsibility to a human being, to flesh and blood. What was the responsibility given to Peter that was signified by the keys? The language of 'binding' and 'loosing' is a Jewish expression and it refers to teaching authority. Jewish rabbis had authority to bind and loose the Jewish law, to declare which parts of the law were binding and which could be interpreted loosely. What Jesus is portrayed as doing in our gospel reading today is giving Peter responsibility for interpreting, not the Jewish law, but the teaching of Jesus for the members of the church.

Jesus was willing to entrust enormous responsibility to human beings. He may have given special responsibility to Peter, but he also entrusted great responsibility to all his followers. At the very end of Mathew's gospel he called on all his disciples to go forth and make disciples of all the nations. In the Our Father we pray, 'Thy kingdom come.' We, thereby, recognise that the coming of God's kingdom is primarily God's responsibility.

We look to God to see to the coming of God's kingdom. Yet, there is a great deal in the gospels to suggest that the coming of God's kingdom is also our responsibility. Jesus has made the coming of God's kingdom, the promotion of God's values, dependant on all of us – on some more than on others, certainly, but on all the baptised. Jesus was taking a tremendous risk in doing this. Peter, who was given the greatest responsibility, left a lot to be desired. In next Sunday's gospel reading, which follows immediately after our gospel reading today, Jesus turns to Peter and says, 'Get behind me Satan.' The rock on which the church was built immediately became an instrument of Satan. Yet, there is no indication in the gospel that Jesus then took back the responsibility he had given to Peter. Jesus presumably knew that he was dealing with very fickle instruments, and yet he entrusted enormous responsibility to them.

Most of us are reasonably aware of our own failings and limitations; the older we get, the more aware we become of them. In spite of our weaknesses, Jesus continues to entrust us with responsibility for the coming of God's kingdom on earth. What else can he do? We are all he has. The choirs of angels cannot do the job he wants done. It is a job for flesh and blood, for flawed people who are, nevertheless, generous, and who learn to trust the Lord as much as he trusts them. When it comes to doing the work of the Lord, whatever that might mean for any one of us, we are not on our own. The Lord is with us. We have his word for it. 'I will be with you always until the end of the age'. The Lord will work within us and among us, if we grasp the responsibility he has given us. That is clear even from today's gospel reading. When Peter made his marvellous confession, Jesus said to him, 'It was not flesh and blood that revealed this to you, but my Father in heaven.' Jesus was saying to him, 'Well done, but it was not all your doing.' It is never all our doing. If we do what only we can do, God will certainly do what only God can do.

Twenty Second Sunday of the Year

Most of us have to deal with a certain amount of conflict in our lives from time to time. Sometimes the conflict can be over something relatively minor and it gets resolved easily and we move on from it quickly. At other times, the conflict can be about something very important. Fundamental issues can be involved, and the fall out from the conflict can be much more serious.

The gospel reading this morning portrays a moment of real conflict between Jesus and Peter. The one whom Jesus had just declared to be the rock on which he would build his church, he now addresses as a stumbling stone. Simon, to whom Jesus had given the name 'Peter' or 'Rock', is now named 'Satan' or 'adversary'. How quickly a moment of great communion between Jesus and Simon became a moment of very serious conflict. If we reflect on this conflict as outside observers, we can see what was going on easily enough. Jesus spoke a truth that Peter found difficult to accept. Jesus spoke out of a strong sense of reality, whereas Peter responded out of a desire to protect Jesus at all costs, and probably himself as well. What Jesus said was shaped by God's way of thinking, what Peter said was shaped by a very human way of thinking.

Perhaps that is why we can so readily identify with Peter. He thinks and speaks as we tend to think and speak. In today's gospel we can all sympathise with the struggle in Peter to face up to a very painful reality. We all have a tendency to protect ourselves and those we care about from bad news. We hold back from speaking a truth that we know is going to be difficult for someone to hear. We ourselves have a way of not hearing what is painful to hear. Sometimes our inability or unwillingness to hear what we need to hear but do not want to hear can bring us into conflict with others. The person who brings us this painful news can easily become the problem, and we can fail to see that the problem is more within ourselves. Reality can be hard to bear. Jesus' reply to Peter in today's gospel reading – 'the way you think is not God's way but man's' – suggests that God's way is the way that faces up to reality, and that God is always to be found in the truth, however painful that truth might be.

It was God's way, or God's will, that Jesus should remain

faithful to his mission of preaching the gospel of God's kingdom, even if this led to Jesus being put to death on a cross. This
was the painful reality that Peter found hard to accept and that
he reacted so strongly to. It is also God's will that we ourselves
remain faithful followers of his Son, even though this will often
mean taking the more difficult path. Jesus declares in today's
gospel that following him will sometimes mean renouncing ourselves and taking up our cross, as he had to do. The language
Jesus uses of renouncing ourselves if we are to be his followers
does not have much of a contemporary ring to it. Self-renunci-
ation is not really in vogue. You could argue that what is more in
vogue in today's culture is self-promotion and self-fulfilment.
Yet, it is very much the gospel message that it is in giving that
we receive, it is in reaching beyond ourselves for the sake of
Christ that we ultimately find ourselves. In the words of the
gospel reading, 'Anyone who loses his life for my sake will find
it.' A way of putting that in more contemporary terms is that we
find happiness, not by looking for happiness directly, but by
reaching towards something more fundamental than happiness,
namely, the kind of generous service of God and neighbour that
Jesus demonstrated by his way of life.

We will often find a resistance within ourselves to this call to
reach beyond ourselves for the sake of the Lord, the kind of resistance we find in Peter and in Jeremiah in today's readings.
Peter said, 'Lord, this must not happen to you.' Jeremiah said, 'I
will not think about him anymore.' Such reactions are very understandable. Yet, both of them overcame their resistances.
Jeremiah spoke about a fire burning in his heart which he simply
could not ignore. There is something of that fire burning in all of
us; it is the fire of God's Spirit, the fire of love urging us to give
ourselves to the service of the Lord and his people. The gospel
reading today suggests that it is only in attending to this fire and
keeping it burning that we will find true happiness.

Twenty-Third Sunday of the Year

I am sure that most of us could name people who influenced us for the better in the course of our lives. Many of us will think of our parents or, perhaps, some teacher or a good friend or a football coach. These are people who helped to bring the best out in us. They took an interest in us; they encouraged us when we needed encouragement, and challenged us when we were losing the run of ourselves. Their challenging word was probably more difficult to hear than their encouraging word, but deep down we knew that both sets of words were coming from the same source, from a heart that cared and was interested.

In the story of Cain and Abel in the book of Genesis, after Cain killed Abel, the Lord said to Cain, 'Where is your brother?' and Cain replied, 'I do not know; am I my brother's keeper?' That question of Cain has echoed down through the ages, 'Am I my brother's or sister's keeper?' 'Am I responsible for others?' The message of the gospel is very clear. In a very fundamental way, we are responsible for each other. We need, in a sense, to be looking out for each other. That strong gospel value is evident in the gospel reading today. A clear procedure is offered there for dealing with a member of the church, a fellow traveller in faith, who has gone off the rails. It is taken for granted that if someone is on a self-destructive course, it is the responsibility of everyone in the community to somehow bring that person to his or her senses. The particular procedure for doing that, which the gospel reading suggests, is not necessarily one that we might be inclined to adopt today. However, what remains valid for us today is that, as fellow pilgrims, we are, to some extent, responsible for each other. None of us journeys to God alone. We travel that journey together, and we are dependant on each other to travel it well. As believers, we need the encouragement and the challenge that only other believers can provide.

It is sobering to realise that we are called to bring each other to the Lord. The Lord works through each of us to touch the lives of others, to draw others to him. In a sense, the Lord has made himself dependent on us. Yet, we are aware that as well as leading each other to the Lord, we can also block each other from making deeper contact with the Lord. Any one of us can become a stumbling stone for another, or for several others. We can bring each other to the Lord or lead each other away from him. That is the awesome influence and responsibility that we have. In the gospels, Jesus is quite severe on those who prove a stumbling stone to others: 'If any of you put a stumbling stone before one of these little ones who believe in me, it would be better for you if a great millstone were fastened around your neck and you were drowned in the depth of the sea.'

We need to be mindful of the influence that we have on each other's relationship with the Lord – an influence that can be for good or for bad. In the first reading, the prophet Ezekiel was appointed as a sentry to the House of Israel. A sentry stood on the walls of the city, ready to warn the citizens of any approaching danger. It was a responsible job, because the welfare of others was dependent on his doing it well. There is a sense in which we are all called to be sentries, people who look out for each other's well being – and not just each other's physical well being, but each other's moral and spiritual well being as well. The first step in attending to each other's well being, in this broad sense, is to attend to our own well being. When I respond generously to the Lord's call in my own life, I am building up the faith of those around me. When I turn away from the Lord's call, I am undermining their faith. When I fail to live the values of the gospel, I am making it more difficult for others to do so. When I strive to live the values of the gospel, I am helping others to do the same, even if my living of the gospel appears to be bearing little fruit in others. Sometimes it is not given to us to see the fruit of our own efforts. Yet, we can be confident that to the extent that we allow Christ to live in us, we will also be creating a space for him to live in others.

Twenty-Fourth Sunday in Ordinary Time

When the relationship between two individuals or two communities breaks down, it generally takes time for healing and reconciliation to occur. The deeper the hurt involved, the more time is needed. The journey can be slow and difficult. It was C. S. Lewis who said, 'Everyone says forgiveness is a lovely idea, until they have someone to forgive.' We may be able to go a certain distance towards reconciliation reasonably quickly, but completing the journey will often take a lot of time.

In the parable that Jesus speaks in today's gospel reading, the servant who owed the king a huge amount of money pleaded, 'Give me time and I will pay you.' Another servant who owed this first servant a relatively small some of money pleaded with him in the same words, 'Give me time and I will pay you.' Both of them asked for time to put right a wrong they had done, to pay a debt that they owed. We need to give each other the gift of time, because it often takes time for people to come right. In the parable, however, neither of the two servants was given the time that they asked for. The king simply cancelled the huge debt of the first servant there and then. Time was dispensed with. The first servant had the second servant thrown into prison, with the result that he was deprived of the time that he needed to repay the debt.

In this parable, Jesus appears to be drawing a sharp contrast between the way God relates to us and the way we often relate to each other. As the prophet Isaiah declared: '"My thoughts are not your thoughts, nor are your ways my ways", says the Lord.' In the parable, when both servants asked for time, they were thinking in terms of work. They needed time to work off what they owed. However, the king gave the servant what he was looking for before he had time to work for it. The parable suggests that God does not ask us to work for the mercy that we need. The forgiveness that God extends to us when we sin is not a response to our efforts. Jesus reveals a God who gives generously to those who have nothing to offer. It can be difficult for us to comprehend the extent to which God is 'for us'. We can easily slip into the way of thinking that is expressed in the plea of the servant, 'Give me time.' God has given us something much more precious than time. God has given and continues to give us his Son, and that extraordinary gift makes the gift of time superfluous. We do not need to ask God, 'Give me time.'

Yet, we very often need to make this request of each other. The second servant's request to his fellow-servant, 'Give me time', was a perfectly reasonable request. The first servant, having been given much more from the king than he had asked for, should have granted his fellow-servant the time that he needed. The parable suggests that the least we might do is to give each other the gift of time – given how much we have received and continue to receive from God. We can be tempted to refuse this gift, cutting people who have hurt us out of our lives, as the servant had his fellow servant thrown into prison. We can, in a sense, imprison each other by our unwillingness to rise above the hurt that has been done to us. The first reading today speaks about nursing anger and cherishing resentment. Anger and even resentment are normal human emotions. If we are alive at all we will inevitably experience them. What is not inevitable is that we nurse and cherish those feelings. We can allow ourselves to become too attached to the hurt that may have been done to us, and also to the anger and resentment that the hurt generates. They can become like cherished possessions which we are unwilling to surrender.

Letting go of these cherished possessions can be difficult. Learning to forgive, 'from the heart', in the words of today's gospel reading, can be a real struggle. Forgiving from the heart is really only possible with God's help. It is only God who can change our heart. It is only in relationship with God that we can begin to move from resentment to forgiveness. As we grow in our appreciation of the mercy that God has shown us and continues to show us though his Son, we will find it more and more difficult to withhold from others what we have been so generously given. The more we recognise ourselves as forgiven sinners, the harder it will be to refuse the gift of time to those who have sinned against us.

Twenty-Fifth Sunday in Ordinary Time

For most of us, our day to day life can be reasonably predictable. One day is much the same as the day before. We have a certain routine that we tend to keep to. Many of us do not like our routine to be disturbed. However, we also know from experience that the unexpected can suddenly come along and throw our routine up into the air. Some misfortune can strike us or those we love and nothing is ever quite the same again. Or, alternatively, wonderful news can come to us out of the blue and everything we subsequently do is bathed in a new light.

That element of the unexpected is very present in today's gospel reading. There is something very surprising, even shocking, about the way that the landowner in that story operates. Most employers do not give the equivalent of a day's wage to somebody who only does an hour's work. If they did, their business would not last very long. Why would anyone want to work for a day if they were given a day's wages for an hour's work? The story that Jesus tells is decidedly not about the human way of doing things. Rather, in story form, Jesus is giving us a picture of God's way of doing things, and God's way of doing things is very different from our way. As the Lord says in today's first reading: 'My thoughts are not your thoughts, my ways are not your ways.' Because God's ways are not our ways, we will often find God surprising and even disconcerting, as listeners to the parable today continue to find the behaviour of the landowner disconcerting.

We know from experience that people can surprise us; they do not always behave as we might expect them to. Some people might surprise us in a negative sense. They do not measure up to our legitimate expectations of them; they disappoint us. Others can surprise us in a positive sense. They far exceed our expectations; they show us that there is more to them than we ever realised. Today's parable suggests that God will surprise us in that positive sense. God's goodness is always greater than we realise; God's generosity far exceeds our expectations – indeed, can never be contained by human expectations. God does not give to us in accordance with what we have earned. God does not calculate how much we have done and then treat us accordingly. God does not put our efforts on one side of the scale and then put an equal amount of God's favour on the other side of the scale to balance our efforts. God's mind and heart work on a far greater and more generous scale that is normal among human beings. Sometimes we can imagine God in all too human terms. In our way of relating to others we tend to give in proportion to what we receive, to love those who love us, to bestow our favour on those who have been good to us. However, today's parable declares that God is not a more powerful version of ourselves; God is fundamentally different; God graces us in unexpected and undeserved ways.

When we reflect on it, most of the best things in life are unearned; they are simply given. Nature in all its beauty and grandeur is given to us; we have not put it together; it is there to be received and, of course, respected. The human experience of being looked upon in love by another is not something we earn. We are graced by the unexpected gift of someone's friendship and love. In a similar way, God's favour, God's love is given, not earned. We are loved by God, before we do anything, because God is Love, and God does not take back that love, regardless of what we do or fail to do. As it has been said, 'God does not work from the arithmetic of the calculator, but from the fullness of God's own heart.' The gospels, and especially today's parable, even suggest that God has a slight prejudice in favour of life's latecomers, those who take a while to get going. There is an extravagance about God's generosity that could make us angry if we were prone to envy but is ultimately very consoling and reassuring. Indeed, true followers of Jesus are so appreciative of God's goodness in their own lives that they are never envious of God's goodness towards others.

We are each challenged to reflect something of God's indiscriminate goodness and generosity in our dealings with one another. The God of surprising generosity can become palpable for others in and through our own way of relating. God's ways are indeed not our ways, but our ways can become a little more like God's ways.

Twenty-Sixth Sunday in Ordinary Time

Most of us get annoyed when people say they will do something for us and then fail to deliver on their promise. Yet, if we are honest with ourselves, we will recognise that we all fail in this respect. There is something of the second son in today's parable in all of us, the son who told his father he would work in the vineyard, but never did so. Our 'yes' can become a 'no' in practice. There can be many reasons for this. We may say 'yes' just to keep someone happy, without ever really intending to follow up on what we are asked. Or some of us may find it hard to say 'no'. We may tend to say 'yes' to every request and have the intention to follow through, even though we could not possibly do all we promise to do.

If there can be something of the second son in all of us, there can also be something of the first son in us as well. I am sure you have had the experience of saying 'no' to some request, and then, having thought it over, you changed your mind. Our first reactions are not always our best ones. They do not always express what, deep down, we really intend. We all struggle with various forms of self-centredness, and sometimes our initial 'no' comes out of that. We might initially say 'no' to avoid what we think will be difficult or demanding. Yet, when we think back over our 'no', we come to realise that it has not done us justice. We recognise that saying 'yes' would be more in keeping with what we desire in the depths of our being.

It is this willingness to change our 'no' into a 'yes' that Jesus is trying to encourage by means of the parable of the two sons. It is addressed to those who have said 'no' to John the Baptist and to Jesus and who show no sign of changing their 'no' into a 'yes'. The religious leaders had not only rejected the appeal of John and Jesus, but having seen how tax collectors and prostitutes had responded generously to John and Jesus, they refused to 'think better of' their 'no'. They persisted in saying 'no' to God's invitation, even though something was happening which should have given them reasons to reconsider their initial negative response. The parable indicates that the Lord is not put off by an initial 'no'. What does trouble him is a persistent 'no', an ongoing refusal to reconsider our initial negative response.

Indeed, the parable suggests that the Lord can put up with a lot of 'no's on the way to a final 'yes'. He is prepared to keep on knocking, as long as there is some prospect that sooner or later we will respond.

There are many examples of people in the gospel story whose 'no' to the Lord's call was not the last word. Nicodemus initially rejected Jesus' call to allow himself to be born again of water and the Spirit. However, by the end of John's gospel, we find him in the company of Joseph of Arimathea, helping to arrange a dignified burial for Jesus. Nathanael's initial reaction to Jesus, 'Can anything good come out of Nazareth?' was not to be his final word. He goes on to confess Jesus as 'the Son of God, the King of Israel'. Moving beyond the time of Jesus, Augustine's early life amounted to a strong 'no' to the values of the gospel that his mother Monica held out to him. After many years, however, his persistent 'no' turned into a 'yes'. Many years later again, when he reflected back on his life, he wrote: 'Late have I loved thee, Beauty so ancient and so new, late have I loved thee.' The gospels proclaim that it is never too late to change for the better.

That is a message which we all need to hear. Whatever 'no's we may have said in the past need not determine our present or future responses. Each day is a new day, a new opportunity to say 'yes' to the Lord's call as it comes to us through those among whom we live and work. Every 'today' is a new opportunity to think better of something and to make a more generous response to God's call. Each day is an opportunity to put on the 'mind of Christ' that St Paul speaks about in our second reading. That mind of Christ shows itself in a willingness to put the interests of others before our own, just as Christ emptied himself for the sake of us all. It is never too late to grow more fully into the mind and heart of Christ. God is prepared to wait.

Twenty-Seventh Sunday in Ordinary Time

Most of us will have experienced disappointment at some time in our lives. Something we put effort into did not work out as we had hoped. More often than not, it is other people who disappoint us. We invest something of ourselves in people. We have some expectations of them on the basis of that. They let us down.

Most of us learn to live with that experience of being disappointed by others. The realisation that we ourselves have probably disappointed others many times may help us to accept others who disappoint us. It can happen, however, that the repeated experience of disappointment can leave us discouraged and disheartened. We retreat into ourselves and settle for less. We become slow to trust and disinclined to give too much. Learning to deal well with the experience of disappointment in ways that do not diminish us is one of the tasks and challenges of life.

The first reading and the gospel reading today shine a light on the experience of disappointment. In the first reading, a vineyard owner is disappointed by his vineyard. In spite of generous investment of work and resources on his part, the vineyard offered him back sour grapes instead of good grapes. Although the parable Jesus speaks also focuses on the disappointment of a vineyard owner, the experience of disappointment it explores is much more traumatic and painful. Here the disappointment of the landowner is not with his land but with the people to whom he entrusted his land. Not only do the tenants not offer him the produce of the land, they maim and kill the messengers he sent in his name, including his own son. The story Jesus tells has a sinister element not present in the sad song that Isaiah sings.

The sad song and the story of betrayal and murder both give expression to God's disappointment with his people. God has invested heavily in us. God has given us his Son and has poured the Spirit of his Son into our hearts. Yet, the first reading and gospel reading bring home to us the uncomfortable truth that our lives do not always bear the kind of fruit that such an investment has a right to expect. We do not always fulfil God's hopes for us.

Where does that leave us? I suggest it leaves us on our knees asking God to help us to open up our hearts to the many gifts God is always giving us, so that those gifts can truly shape our lives and make of them a gift to God and God's people. In the second reading, Paul encourages us: 'There is no need to worry; but if there is anything you need, pray for it, asking God for it with prayer and thanksgiving.' Paul himself knew that he had disappointed God. He may have had little difficulty identifying with the tenants in today's parable who killed the landowner's son. Writing to the Corinthians, he states: 'For I am the least of the apostles, unfit to be called an apostle, because I persecuted the church of God.' Yet, he immediately goes on to add: 'But by the grace of God I am what I am, and his grace towards me has not been in vain.' Paul knew from experience that God continues to invest in us even after we have failed and disappointed him.

Jesus reveals a God who works to bring new life out of our failures, who can turn a rejected stone into a keystone. We catch glimpses of this God in those who continue to journey with us even when we have repeatedly disappointed them. We reveal this God to others when we ourselves keep faith with those who give us little reason to go on believing in them.

The conviction that God remains faithful to us even after we have disappointed him many times does not leave us complacent. Rather, this conviction keeps fresh our desire to live lives that are full of the fruit of the Holy Spirit. It encourages us to keep seeking the Lord whose power at work within us can do immeasurably more than all we can ask or imagine. Seeking the Lord entails filling 'our minds with everything that is true, everything that is noble, everything that is good and pure ... everything that can be thought virtuous or worthy of praise'. A lot of talent, effort and money are invested in filling our minds and hearts with rubbish. Yet, we have choices. We can decide in what ways our minds and hearts will be filled. We can make the kinds of choices that will create a space for God's continued investment in us to bear rich fruit, both in our own lives and in the lives of those with whom we journey.

Twenty-Eighth Sunday in Ordinary Time

We sometimes refer light-heartedly to the person who makes someone an offer they cannot refuse. We are aware of the paradox in that statement. To offer an invitation implies leaving people free to accept the invitation or not. An offer or an invitation that cannot be refused is not an offer or an invitation in any true sense of the word.

The parable in today's gospel reading tells the story of a king who offered an invitation to his son's wedding feast that was refused by many. In that culture people normally received two invitations to a feast, an initial invitation some time before the event, and a second one just as the meal was ready. To refuse the second invitation, having already said yes to the first invitation, would have been a great insult to the host. It is this second invitation that people decline in the parable that we have just heard. The equivalent situation today might be someone who had accepted an invitation to a meal in a friend's house and then, just ten minutes before the meal is due to start, rings up and says he or she will not be able to come after all.

In the parable, the king who invites people to the wedding feast of his son is an image of God who invites people to join his Son, Jesus. John the Baptist once referred to himself as the friend of the bridegroom. God invites all of us to become friends of the bridegroom, to join Jesus at table, to become his companions, to enter into communion with him and to live out of that. This is the great Christian calling, the great invitation that God extends to all men and women. The fact that this calling is expressed in the terms of an invitation to a wedding feast suggests that there is a real celebratory element to this calling. It is a call to joy, not a superficial joy, but the deep-seated joy that comes from knowing that God values us so much that he desperately wants us to be present at his Son's great feast.

There is joy at the heart of the Christian life. The life, death and resurrection of Jesus give us something to celebrate, even when life is going against us. Jesus' life, death and resurrection proclaim the good news that God's mercy is stronger than our sin, that God's life is stronger than our various experiences of death, that God's power is stronger than our weakness. We can say with St Paul in today's second reading: 'There is nothing I cannot master with the help of the One who gives me strength.' Paul wrote that letter from his prison cell. He had been through a great deal, and he suspected that worse was to come, and yet that little letter is full of joy. Even though it was written out of a real Calvary experience, it radiates the light of Easter. We always live and walk in the light of Easter, even in our darkest moments. The Christian calling is to be joyful and hopeful. It is a calling to live as people who are convinced that, whatever happens to us in life, in the words of today's responsorial psalm, God's goodness and kindness shall follow us all the days of our lives, until we finally come to that great banquet spoken about in today's first reading at which death will be destroyed forever.

That joyful, hopeful living that God calls us to is not a way of life that leaves us self-satisfied and smug. On the contrary, an authentically joyful and hopeful life will always overflow into service of others. In carrying the joy and hope of the gospel in our hearts, we are moved to bring joy where there is sadness, hope where there is despair, courage to the fearful, companionship to the lonely, acceptance to those who have experienced rejection. This is the wedding garment that is referred to in the parable of today's gospel reading. Those who have been invited to the wedding feast of the Lamb must dress accordingly, live accordingly. Paul in his prison could say to his beloved Philippians: 'It was good of you to share with me in my hardship.' The Philippians journeyed with Paul in his struggles. They knew how to wear their wedding garment.

Each day we are invited to taste the joy and the hope of the gospel for ourselves, and to become messengers of that joy and hope to others. The Eucharist which we celebrate is a concrete expression of the wedding banquet of Christ to which God invites us. At the Sunday Eucharist, we gather to renew our joyful hope and to commit ourselves afresh to joyful and hopeful service of others.

Twenty-Ninth Sunday in Ordinary Time

Image is very important in our media-conscious age. How people look can make a bigger impact than what they say. Yet, we are aware that image is not everything. We expect people to live up to the image they present. We look to people to be authentic, and we tend to value authenticity more than image.

In today's gospel reading, Jesus is approached by people who begin by flattering him: 'Master, we know that you are an honest man and that you teach the way of God in an honest way.' Yet, their flattery was deceptive, because their real intent was to trap Jesus, to get him to say something that would leave him at odds either with the people or with the Roman authorities. Their friendly and flattering image was a cover for great hostility. The image did not correspond to the reality.

When Jesus requested a coin from the pockets of his questioners, he asked them, 'Whose image and inscription is this?' The coin had an image of the emperor on it. Behind that image was the reality that this coin belonged to the emperor and should be given to him, and so Jesus said: 'Give back to Caesar what belongs to Caesar.' However, Jesus immediately goes on to say: 'and (give) to God what belongs to God.' We might well ask: 'If the coin with its image of the emperor belongs to the emperor, what is it that belongs to God?' Behind the statement of Jesus, 'give to God what belongs to God', is the understanding that each one of us bears the image of God, and that, therefore, it is we ourselves who belong to God. Jesus was reminding his questioners that, whereas the coin in their pockets belongs to the emperor, they themselves belong to God, and they must live and behave as people who belong to God. They must give themselves first and foremost to God, and not to the emperor or anyone else.

Because we are God's image, we belong to God, and we strive to live our lives accordingly. We are called to live as people who bear God's image. What we owe to God is far more fundamental than what we owe to anyone else. The gospel reading proclaims that the basic loyalty in our lives must be to God. In the words of today's first reading: 'I am the Lord, unrivalled; there is no other God besides me.'

Every other human loyalty is subordinate to that fundamental loyalty. We owe allegiance to the state, but we owe a greater allegiance to God as Jesus has revealed God. As Christians, our primary allegiance is to the values that Jesus proclaimed and lived. It can happen that people's allegiance to the gospel puts them in conflict with the state. That was certainly true of the time of Jesus and of the time when the evangelists were writing their gospels. In more recent times, many Christians who refused to submit to the ideology of the Nazi state were put to death. The great Protestant pastor and theologian, Dietrich Bonheoffer, and the Catholic priest, Maximillian Kolbe, come to mind.

We are unlikely to suffer that same fate in the state in which we live today. The freedom of religion and worship is enshrined in our constitution. Today, the pressure on us to compromise the values of the gospel comes less from the state and more from the culture in which we live. We can find ourselves under all kinds of subtle pressures to buy into ways of doing things that are in conflict with the values of the gospel. As people who belong to God, we are called to give all areas of our lives to God, to allow God and his Son to shape who we are. Yet, the culture of which we are a part can attempt to put a very different shape on some areas of our lives.

When Paul wrote to the members of the church in Thessalonica, he was aware that they were under this same kind of pressure. Yet, at the beginning of his letter, he remembers with gratitude their faith in action, their work of love and their persevering hope. These early Christians can be our model and inspiration. They show us that we can give to God what belongs to God, even when under pressure to do otherwise. We can give to God in this way because of all that God has given to us. In the words of the first reading, God has called us by our name. Furthermore, God has given his Son to us and at this Eucharist we receive anew this great gift. Strengthened by this ongoing gift that God makes to us, we are enabled to give to God all that belongs to God.

Thirtieth Sunday in Ordinary Time

Life is becoming increasingly complex. We value people who have the gift of getting beyond the many dimensions of an issue and who can zoom in on the heart of the matter. Such people prevent us from missing the wood for the trees. They are good at separating out what really matters from what is less important. They encourage us to invest our energies in what is really worthwhile, rather than allowing them to be dissipated by what is not significant.

Jesus was a person who knew how to go to the heart of the matter. On one occasion someone asked him to intervene in a family dispute about inheritance. In his reply, he ignored the concrete issue and, instead, he called on the person who approached him to 'Be on your guard against all kinds of greed' (Lk 12:13-15). He saw that the real issue was not the details of the particular case but the greed that underlay the dispute.

This capacity of Jesus to get to the heart of the matter is clear from his response to the question put to him by one of the Pharisees in today's gospel reading: 'Master, which is the greatest commandment of the Law?' In the time of Jesus there were known to be 613 commandments in the Jewish Law. The potential to miss the wood for the trees was enormous. Preoccupation with the sheer number and detail of regulations could result in people ignoring what really matters. On one occasion Jesus humorously refers to this as straining out a gnat but swallowing a camel. Jesus took advantage of the Pharisee's question to go straight to the heart of the Jewish law. He was asked only about the 'greatest' commandment. His answer, however, named the greatest and the second greatest commandment. For Jesus, the greatest commandment, 'You must love the Lord your God with all your heart, with all your soul, with all your mind', was inseparable from the second greatest commandment, 'You must love your neighbour as yourself.' Jesus' answer declared that what God wants from us above all else is love. Our love is due first to God, but there is no genuine love of God unless it finds expression in love of our neighbour. Love of neighbour, in turn, presupposes a healthy self-love, recognising and appreciating myself as fundamentally good, because I am created in the image and likeness of God.

A few chapters further on in Matthew's gospel, Jesus states that those who live the second greatest commandment can find themselves living the greatest commandment, without realising it. 'Lord when was it that we saw you hungry and gave you food, or thirsty and gave you something to drink … a stranger and welcomed you?' To this question comes the reply: 'Truly I tell you, just as you did it to one of the least of these, you did it to me.' To love the neighbour, especially the vulnerable neighbour, is to love the Lord.

The opening of this morning's first reading mentions several vulnerable neighbours. The first one referred to is the 'stranger'. The term 'stranger' has quite a precise meaning in the scriptures. It does not simply refer to people who are not known to us. Parents often rightly tell their children not to take a lift from strangers, in this sense. The term 'stranger' in the scriptures refers to someone from outside Israel who lived in Israel, a foreigner living among the people of Israel. In Ireland in recent years we have moved, and are still in the process of moving, from a mono-cultural society to a multi-cultural and multi-racial society. Today's readings invite us to reflect on how well we have learned to love these strangers, to make them feel at home in our society and in our church. 'I was a stranger and you welcomed me.'

The call to love the stranger can also be heard as a call to love what we find strange in others. As we go through life, we become aware that other people are not extensions of ourselves. They are distinct from us, and often very different from us. It is tempting to frequent the company of people like ourselves. Yet, the Lord gathered about himself a community of great diversity. Even within the twelve there was to be found a tax-collector and a zealot, men with very different attitudes to the keeping of the Jewish law. In a similar way, the Spirit of the Lord at work in our lives prompts us to connect with those who are different from us, as well as those who are like us. The one we find initially strange can reveal the Lord to us in surprising ways. We pray this morning for a greater openness to the many ways the Lord comes to us in life.

Thirty-First Sunday in Ordinary Time

Most of us will feel burdened by life at one time or another. Many of life's burdens are inevitable and unavoidable. Ill health in ourselves or in those we love will be experienced as a burden. Some of the tasks we find ourselves having to do will often be burdensome. Young people find examinations a burden. The list could go on and on. The experience of being burdened is an inevitable part of life.

Yet, each of us has the capacity to make life more burdensome or less burdensome for others. In Matthew's gospel, Jesus called out to the people, 'Come to me, all you who are wearied and are carrying heavy burdens, and I will give you rest.' In today's gospel reading, the source of those heavy burdens is identified. Jesus criticises the Pharisees because 'they tie up heavy burdens and lay them on people's shoulders', without lifting a finger to move them. The teachers of religion have taken the message of the liberating power of God's love and recast it into a series of burdens that those they instruct are forced to carry. The God whom Jesus reveals makes life less burdensome. The God whom some of the religious leaders in Jesus' day revealed made life more burdensome. They have been hiding the God that Jesus came to reveal.

Today's gospel reveal is a challenge to religious leaders of every generation. It invites those in positions of pastoral leadership to ask: 'Does the way we proclaim the gospel reveal the life-giving power of the living God, or does it add to the burdens people are already carrying?' Revelations about clerical sexual abuse in recent years and how church authorities have dealt with them have been hugely burdensome for many people. Many feel that the church, to which they looked as a supportive presence on their life's journey, has let them down. The burden of disillusionment this has created for many people cannot be underestimated.

All of us in the church, and not just those in positions of pastoral leadership, are challenged by the example of Paul, the great pastor, that is put before us in today's second reading. He tells the Thessalonians that 'We felt so devoted and protective towards you, that we were ... slaving night and day so as not to be a burden on any one of you while we were proclaiming God's good news to you.' Paul proclaimed the gospel by his words and by his life, revealing it to be, not a burden, but a 'living power among you who believe it'. The living power of the gospel is the living power of God's kingdom. The whole church, the members of Christ's body, is called to be at the service of God's kingdom. We are to be a living sign of God's kingdom in the world. Because the kingdom of God is a much more wonderful reality than the church, and yet the church is called to be a sacrament of that kingdom, all of us in the church are always in need of ongoing renewal and reform. The renewal and reform of the church will take different forms at different times in its history.

In today's gospel reading, Jesus tells us that 'you have only one Father, and he is in heaven ... you have only one Teacher, the Christ.' Even though we may address people as 'father' in a family context and in a church context, and address people as 'teacher' in a school or college context, today's gospel reminds us that there is only one who is truly worthy of the title 'Father', namely God, and only one who is truly worthy of the title 'Teacher', namely Christ. Every 'father' and 'teacher' is called to be a sacrament, a living sign, of the one 'Father' and the one 'Teacher', just as the church is called to be the sacrament of the kingdom.

None of us have had perfect fathers or perfect teachers in life. At times our fathers and our teachers may have burdened us unnecessarily, or even damaged us. Yet, although our earthly fathers and teachers may fail us, our heavenly Father and our wise Teacher will not fail us. God and his Son continue to serve us in love, bringing us new life, directing our way. In today's responsorial psalm, the psalmist, aware of the limitations of the human condition, surrenders to God, as a weaned child on its mother's breast. This surrender is an expression of his hope, hope in the Lord whose faithfulness endures forever. When we are brought face to face with our own limitations as disciples and the limitations of others in the church, we are given an opportunity to surrender more fully to the Lord who continues to work among us.

Thirty-Second Sunday in Ordinary Time

It is lovely to be met by someone when we arrive home from a journey. It makes all the difference to be greeted by a familiar face. To be met by a friendly face is all the more gratifying if our arrival has been delayed. As the minutes tick by, we wonder if the friend who promised to meet us will still be there when we arrive. Doubting their presence, we might find ourselves thinking about other, less convenient, ways of negotiating the last, short stage of the journey. Recognising the hoped-for presence in the crowd, despite our very late arrival, makes us all the more appreciative of their coming. Our delay has changed nothing. They have been true to their word, in spite of the inconvenience of the unexpected delay.

Perhaps the bridegroom, in today's gospel reading, was equally pleased to find that at least some of the bridesmaids were there to meet and escort him to the wedding banquet, in spite of his very late arrival. The darkness would be lit up with bright lights after all. The faithfulness of at least some of the bridesmaids was all the more appreciated, because it required foresight and attentiveness.

We value faithfulness in others, especially when we know that it has cost them something. We appreciate it when people keep vigil for us, when not to do so would be very understandable. Those who remain at their post, in spite of an unexpected turn of events, are great treasures. It is one thing to be faithful when all goes according to plan. It is another matter to remain faithful when the plan unravels and the situation turns out very differently to what had been expected.

Having finished telling the parable of the ten bridesmaids, Jesus turned to his disciples and said to them, 'Stay awake, because you do not know either the day or the hour.' He was calling on them to be faithful to him, especially during those times when he seemed absent and their expectations were not being realised. When the Lord calls us to be his followers, it is always for the long haul. When he addresses us as 'the light of the world', he looks to us to keep our light burning to the very end. Through baptism, the Lord calls on us to keep the flame of the gospel burning in our hearts and in our lives, so that the light of that flame is there to greet him, regardless of the lateness or strangeness of his coming to us.

In the times in which we live, it can be a struggle to keep the flame of faith alive in our hearts. Like some of those in the gospel reading today, we may find ourselves crying, 'Our lamps are going out.' The flame of faith can grow weak, and we can be tempted to give up watching and waiting. When we sense that the Lord has let us down, or has not responded to our prayers, we can easily loose heart. The enthusiasm we might once have had for the bridegroom can dissipate. Paul was dealing with this kind of situation in our second reading. Some members of the church had died since he was last with them, and many in the church were grieving like people who had no hope. The experience of loss, the pain of the cross, was taking its toll on many. Paul needed to reassure them that the Lord was stronger than death and that one day there would be a great reunion around the Lord – 'We will stay with the Lord forever.'

We all need the same kind of reassurance from time to time. We need help to keep vigil, especially in those times when our faith is put to the test in some way. That help comes from the Lord. The first reading today assures us that 'Wisdom is bright, and does not grow dim.' For us Christ is the Wisdom of God. We are being assured that the light of Christ's presence does not grow dim. Whatever about us, the Lord remains faithful. His faithful presence to us will help to keep our lamps burning and will continue to fan the flame of our faith. What is asked of us is that, in the words of the responsorial psalm, we gaze on him in the sanctuary. We are to keep our focus on the Lord, turning prayerfully towards him, even when he seems to delay in coming.

As followers of Christ, we are called to have a faith that endures. It is the only kind of faith that is worth having. It is the faith that Jesus himself had. If we keep looking to him, he will nurture that same kind of faith in us.

Thirty-Third Sunday in Ordinary Time

We know from experience that different people have different abilities. A person with an ability to listen to others may not have the ability to be a good administrator. Someone who is well able to mend a leak or fix a washing machine may have little or no musical ability. An effective teacher may be a hopeless mechanic. We learn from experience who is good at what, and we relate to people accordingly. We also learn from experience what our own abilities and limitations are, and we tend to take on tasks that correspond to our abilities and avoid tasks that do not.

The rich man in today's parable was well aware of the abilities of his servants. Before he set out on his journey he entrusted his property 'to each in proportion to his ability'. He knew what each of his three servants was able for, and he only gave as much responsibility to each of them as each could carry. The man who received five talents of money was capable of making five more; the one who received two talents was capable of making two more; the one who received one talent was capable of making one more. The first two servants worked according to their ability. The third servant did not, giving his master back the one talent he had been given, instead of the two talents he was capable of acquiring. What held this servant back from working according to his ability was fear. 'I was afraid, and I went off and hid your talent in the ground.'

Many of us may find ourselves having some sympathy for the third servant, because, deep down, we are only too well aware how fear can hold us back and prevent us from doing what we are well capable of doing. Fear can be a much more powerful force in the lives of some than others. Those who have experienced a lot of criticism growing up can be slow to take a risk and may develop a fearful approach to life. An old Irish proverb states, 'Praise the young and they will make progress.' The converse can also true. Criticise the young and they will be held back. Unfair criticism can stunt our growth and prevent us from reaching our God-given potential. We hide what we have been given in the ground. There it remains safe, but useless.

Jesus was only too well aware of the disabling power of fear in people's lives. It is striking the number of times he says, 'Do not be afraid.' When Simon Peter fell down at Jesus' knees saying, 'Depart from me, Lord, for I am a sinful man', Jesus replied to him, 'Do not be afraid, from now on it is people you will catch.' When fear threatened to hold Peter back, Jesus called him forward into a new way of life. Jesus was present to people in ways that released them from their fear. He did not want fear of failure to hold people back. He could cope with failure in others; many people could learn from failure. However, there is little to be learned from staying put. There is much to be learnt from striking out, even if failure is experienced along the way.

The tragedy of the third servant in the parable today is that, out of fear, he hid what had been entrusted to him, even though he had the ability to use it well. We have each been graced in some way by the Lord for the service of others. If I hide what the Lord has given me, others are thereby deprived. Most of us need a bit of encouragement to place our gifts at the disposal of others. Part of our baptismal calling is to give others courage, to encourage others. In these difficult times for the church, the ministry of encouragement is all the more necessary. There is much to be learned from the mistakes of the past. But the Lord would not want us to go to ground. He has entrusted to us the treasure of the gospel. Now is not the time to hide that treasure in the ground out of fear. Rather, it is a time to encourage each other to share what the Lord has given to us, so that the church may become all that God is calling it to be.

In this connection, it is worth calling to mind the words of Nelson Mandela: 'We were born to make manifest the Glory of God that is within us. It's not just in some of us; it's in everyone. And as we let our own Light shine, we unconsciously give other people permission to do the same. As we are liberated from our own fear, our presence automatically liberates others.'

Solemnity of Christ the King

You might have had the experience of doing something for somebody and only subsequently discovering that it meant far more to that person than you realised at the time. We don't always appreciate how significant our actions are for others or how much our presence means to them. That can be a good thing because it prevents us from taking ourselves too seriously. In other ways it may not be a good thing because we can fail to value something in ourselves that others value very much. We may be tempted to give up doing something that people really value because we are unaware of how significant it is.

In today's gospel reading the first group were amazed to discover that what they had done in life was far more significant than they had realised. Only at the end of their lives did they discover that their ordinary simple acts of kindness and consideration were in fact serving the Lord of Lords and King of Kings. To their amazement, they recognised that there was a much deeper dimension to what they were doing than they had ever suspected. In attending to the ordinary, they were in reality engaging with the eternal. 'When did we see you ...' they asked the glorious Son of Man. His reply was, 'In so far as you did this to one of the least, you did it to me.' In dealing with their broken and troublesome and unfortunate neighbours, they were, in reality, dealing with the Lord of the Universe. What they had been doing had consequences far beyond what they realised at the time. The parable suggests that the Lord sees the value of the good we do more clearly than we see it ourselves.

It can be difficult for us to realise that in our ordinary dealings with each other we are in a very real sense dealing with the Lord. It is in the ordinary, every day affairs of life that we meet the Lord. The care that someone gives to a sick relative is care given to the Lord. The welcome we give to a stranger who feels vulnerable in a foreign environment is a welcome given to the Lord. The way we relate to prisoners or ex-prisoners reveals how we relate to the Lord.

At the beginning of Mass we sometimes pray the prayer we call the Confiteor. In that prayer we ask forgiveness for what we have done and what we have failed to do. If the first part of today's parable emphasises the deeper significance of the simple acts of goodness and kindness that we do, the second part of the parable highlights the deeper significance of what we fail to do. The second group are not accused of violent crime or offences on a grand scale – any more than the first group were praised for heroic virtue. They were accused because they failed to respond to the human need they saw before them. Most of us, if we reflect on our lives at all, will be conscious of what we have failed to do. It is common for those who are grieving the loss of a loved one to be troubled with guilt over what they failed to do for their loved ones who have died. Yet, burdening ourselves with guilt over what we have failed to do is not the Lord's will for us. Jesus did not speak this parable to add to the burdens we carry. Rather, the parable is a call to become more attentive to those who are struggling alongside us and to respond to them out of our resources.

The parable calls us to take responsibility for shepherding each other, after the example of Jesus the good shepherd. This is the feast of Christ the King, but if Jesus is a king, he is a shepherd/king. He is the kind of shepherd/king referred to in today's first reading, the one who looks for the lost, brings back the stray, bandages the wounded and makes the weak strong. This is how Jesus relates to all of us, because we are all lost, straying, wounded and weak in various ways. The second reading states that, as king, Jesus goes even further, bringing life to the dead – 'all will be brought to life in Christ'. Today's feast calls on us to relate to each other in the way that our shepherd/king relates to us, to shepherd each other as he shepherds us. St Paul in one of his letters expresses this very well in a prayer he makes: 'Blessed be the God of all consolation, who consoles us in all our affliction, so that we may be able to console those in any affliction with the consolation with which we ourselves are consoled by God.'

Saint Patrick

We venerate Patrick today because he spent himself proclaiming the gospel on this island, bringing Christ to huge numbers of people who never heard of him. Patrick says in his *Confessio*, 'I am very much in debt to God who gave me so much grace that through me many people should be born again in God and afterwards confirmed, and that clergy should be ordained for them everywhere.' In amazement at what God had done through him, he asks: 'How then does it happen in Ireland that a people who in their ignorance of God always worshipped only idols and unclean things up to now, have lately become a people of the Lord and are called children of God?'

Today we give thanks for Patrick's response to God's call to preach the gospel in the land of his former captivity. His first journey to Ireland was not of his own choosing. He was brought here as a slave at the age of 16. This must have been a hugely traumatic experience for a young adolescent. His identity was anything but fully formed at this stage. He says in his confessions: 'I was taken captive ... before I knew what to seek or what to avoid.' This experience was a personal disaster. Yet, out of this traumatic experience came great good. Although Patrick had been baptised a Christian, he had developed no relationship with Christ. The faith into which he had been baptised had made no impact on his life. In his captivity, he had a religious awakening. He tells us: 'When I came to Ireland ... I used to pray many times during the day. More and more the love of God and reverence for him came to me. My faith increased ... As I now realise, the spirit was burning within me.' That spiritual awakening in the land of his captivity had enormous consequences, not only for himself but for huge numbers of people in the land of his captivity.

The Lord somehow got through to Patrick during the rigours of captivity in a way he had not got through to him during his reasonably privileged upbringing at home. Patrick uses a striking image to express this transformation in his life: 'Before I was humbled I was like a stone lying in the deep mud. Then he who is mighty came and in his mercy he not only pulled me out but lifted me up and placed me at the very top of the wall.'

Patrick's own story brings home to us that the Lord can work powerfully in and through our own experiences of captivity. In the course of our lives we can be brought somewhere we would rather not go. We can find ourselves in situations where we are conscious only of loss. We are separated from someone or some place that has been very significant for us. We experience ourselves as isolated and adrift, in unfamiliar territory, unsure of our future and with regrets about the past. Patrick's story reminds us that when we find ourselves in such wilderness places, the Lord does not abandon us. On the contrary, when we seem to be loosing much, he graces us all the more. Patrick says in his confessions: 'I cannot be silent ... about the great benefits and graces that the Lord saw fit to confer on me in the land of my captivity.' The Lord will be as generous with us as he was with Patrick in the land of our captivity, whatever form that might take. If we remain open to the Lord in such times, as Patrick did, the Lord will not only grace us but many others through us.

Many of us in the church are conscious of a sense of loss in recent years. The numbers coming to the sacraments have fallen greatly; there has been a dramatic decline in the numbers going on for priesthood and the religious life; the fabric of our society seems to be more and more resistant to the values of the gospel; the way we have come to relate to each other seem more and more at odds with the Lord's teaching and lifestyle. Patrick's story is a reminder to us that the Lord continues to work powerfully in what appears to be unpromising terrain. In the gospel reading Jesus instructs the seventy two to proclaim the same message regardless of how they are received: 'The kingdom of God is very near to you.' Even in barren and lean times, it remains the case that the kingdom of God is very near to us. Patrick teaches us to be alert to the signs of God's kingdom even in periods of loss. He encourages us to be attentive to the new deed that God is always doing in the land of our captivity.

Feast of the Assumption

Today's feast is a feast of hope. Its meaning is summed up in the words of Mary in the gospel reading: 'The Almighty has done great things for me.' It is a feast which invites us to believe that the Almighty can do great things for all of us, for each of us. Today's feast calls on us to live in the hope of the great things that the Almighty can and will do for us.

In celebrating Mary's assumption, we celebrate the fullness and completeness of life that she now enjoys. The Lord desires that we would all come to that same fullness and completeness of life. We are always conscious of ourselves as incomplete in one way or another. We live with a sense that we are not yet all we could be. Evil, symbolised by the dragon in today's first reading, lurks not only in our world but in our own hearts. We are made in God's image, but we know that we do not always image God as we could. We are not yet all that God intends and desires us to be.

Yet, God has been and still is at work in the lives of each of us, helping us to grow into the image of his Son. Today's feast invites us to believe that God the Almighty who has begun his good work in us will bring that work to completion. That completion will not come to pass in this life; it is only in and through our death that God's work in our lives will be brought to completion. It is only then that every trace of evil in our lives will be taken away and we will be aglow with the glory of God. Whereas Mary, who is fully alive with the fullness of God, can now pray 'The Almighty has done great things for me', our prayer will be a little different because God has not yet fully done the great things God wants to do for us. Our prayer will be more along the lines: 'Lord God Almighty, bring to completion the good work, the great things, you have begun in us.'

Mary has reached the end of her journey, whereas we are still on the way. As today's Preface reminds us, Mary is 'a sign of hope and comfort for your people on their pilgrim way'. As one who has gone before us and now enjoys that fullness and completeness of life for which we all long, we can turn to her and pray: 'Mary, pray for us sinners now and at the hour of our death.' Her prayers can help us now. We look to her now as our

prayerful companion on the way, to help us arrive at that fullness of life she now enjoys. As gloriously assumed into heaven
she is our hope and comfort, but as the simple woman of
Nazareth she can be our model and guide.

In the gospel reading, Elizabeth in response to Mary's greet-
ing declares, 'blessed is she who believed'. Mary was a woman
of faith who listened to God's word and responded to it in her
life. Her whole life was shaped by the response that she made at
the time of the annunciation: 'Let it be to me according to your
word.' It was because she responded to God's call so completely
that God could do great things for her. She was the first believer
and the greatest of all believers. As believers, we look to her to
show us the way, to embody for us what it means to walk
humbly with our God. If we make Mary's priority our own, to
hear God's word and to keep it, then God will be able to complete the good work that God has begun in us, and we will come
to join Mary in that fullness of life that God desires for all of us.
In the words of Paul in today's second reading, we 'will be
brought to life in Christ'.

Feast of the Immaculate Conception

In the technological age in which we live, children's toys have become a great deal more sophisticated than they used to be. Computerised games are more likely to be mentioned in children's letters to Santa than scooters or skipping ropes. Yet, some children's games have endured the test of time and remain as popular now as they were in earlier generations. One such game is the game of hide and seek, where one child hides somewhere and the other children have to search for and find him or her. The enduring popularity of this game that children play may be because it appeals to that quality of the 'seeker' which is deeply rooted in us from a very early age. We enjoy the thrill of the search and the joy of the discovery.

In the game of hide and seek, one of the children must agree to hide if the others are to have the fun of seeking and finding. There are other contexts, especially in adulthood, when hiding ourselves is not so appropriate or praiseworthy. The adult who retreats into himself or herself and puts energy into hiding from others is generally regarded as less than emotionally mature. Such hiding of self can often indicate an unwillingness, or an inability, to face up to one's responsibilities in an adult way. A form of self-hiding that is less observable to others is the hiding of ourselves from God. In today's first reading, Adam is depicted as hiding himself from God. God calls out to him, 'Where are you?' and Adam replies, 'I was afraid because I was naked, so I hid.' God had placed Adam in the Garden of Eden, in a relationship of intimacy with God. Adam had broken that intimate relationship with God by going against God's will. This, in turn, led to Adam hiding from God out of fear and shame.

Many of us may be able to identify with Adam in that first reading. We may have known times when we acted contrary to what we knew in our heart of hearts God was asking of us. As a result, we may have found it difficult to face God. Without, perhaps, making any conscious decision, we may have drifted away from God, unable to face or engage with God, because, at some deep level, we felt unworthy. The first reading suggests that although we may hide from God, God does not hide from us. God continues to call out to us, 'Where are you?' Indeed, in becoming flesh in the person of Jesus, God was saying to us, 'Here I am', and looking for us to respond in kind, 'Here I am.'

In celebrating the feast of Mary's Immaculate Conception, we are celebrating the good news that from the moment of her conception Mary was completely turned towards God. Her whole being proclaimed 'Here I am' from the first moment of her existence. At no time in her life did she feel the need to hide from God. The 'here I am' that she speaks to God in today's gospel reading, 'I am the handmaid of the Lord, let what you have said be done to me', is only the adult expression of a stance before God that she displayed from her very conception. We do not worship Mary as God in human form, as we do Jesus. However, we venerate her as the only human being whose response to God's presence was perfect and complete. Her immaculate conception did not make her perfect response to God's presence easy or trouble free. Today's gospel reading declares that she was 'greatly disturbed' by the words of Gabriel. God's presence and call disturbed the normal rhythm of her life. She would be further and more deeply disturbed by what had yet to unfold: the loss of her Son in the temple, the strange mission of her Son, the death of her Son on a Roman cross. To that extent, her immaculate conception does not remove her from the darker side of the human journey that we all experience.

We see in Mary what we can all become, with God's grace. Today's second reading declares that God has chosen us in Christ to be holy and spotless and to live through love in God's presence. God could not be accused of selling us short. God knows what we can become through the grace of his Son and the power of the Holy Spirit. Mary's life proclaims the truth of Paul's message to the Romans: 'Where sin increased, grace abounded all the more.' Unlike Mary, we will sin. However, God's grace is stronger than our sin and God's love is more enduring than our resistance. We really do not have any reason to hide from God.

Feast of All Saints

A lot of people, probably those of a more introverted nature, do not like large gatherings. They work on the principle that small is beautiful. They find big crowds exhausting and long for space where they can be alone or perhaps with one or two chosen others. Today's feast, however, is precisely about crowds of people. The first reading expresses it well, 'a huge number, impossible to count, of people from every nation, race, tribe and language'. Today is the feast not just of a few chosen saints, but of all saints. It is not even the feast of all the saints who get a mention in the church's calendar of saints. Today we honour all the saints, those who are canonised and those who are not, those who get a mention from time to time in the prayers of the church and those who are never mentioned by name in any liturgy anywhere. When it comes to saints, today's feast is as inclusive as it can get.

Villains are generally considered more newsworthy than saints. If our vision of humanity is shaped exclusively by the media we might be tempted to think that there are a lot more villains out there than saints. In that context, it is reassuring to be reminded that there exists, in reality, a huge number of saints, impossible to count. In the words of the letter to the Hebrews, we are surrounded by a 'great cloud of witnesses'. None of us can live as the Lord is calling us to live on our own. We need the good example of others to encourage us, to inspire us and to show us what is possible. Today's feast declares that we, as followers of Christ, are surrounded by an abundance of role models, if only we could recognise them and pay attention to them. Some of these people have already passed beyond us and are now 'standing in front of the throne of the Lamb', in the words of today's first reading. Many of them, however, are our companions on the journey of life. They are mothers and fathers, single people and celibates, men and women, young and not so young; they are from every nation, race, tribe and language. They do not look at all like the statues in our churches. They are very ordinary and, yet, very special. They are wonderful human beings. They are fully alive and, in virtue of that, they give glory to God. They are attractive and inspiring, loving and challenging, affectionate and strong, gentle and courageous, joyful and serious. We sense that we are the better for having met them and being around them. They could be any one of us. Indeed, they could be all of us, because as John says in today's second reading: 'We are already the children of God.'

The feast of All Saints encourages us to believe that any one of us could be part of the huge number impossible to count. Today's feast is not just about a great crowd of people out there; it is about every one of us. John, in today's second reading, is speaking about all of us when he declares that in the future, 'we shall be like' God. We are all destined for sainthood. God wants us all to be saints; God intends that all of us would be conformed to the image of God's Son. For most of us, that will only happen beyond this life when, in the words of St Paul, our Saviour, the Lord Jesus Christ, will 'transform the body of our humiliation that it may be conformed to the body of his glory'. Yet, because we are already sons and daughters of God, we are called to be growing now towards that wonderful transformation that awaits us. The road to sainthood begins here, wherever we happen to find ourselves.

In today's gospel reading, Jesus shows us what that road looks like. In the beatitudes, Jesus painted a portrait of himself, the living saint *par excellence*. He was also painting a portrait of the person that we are all called to become. The beatitudes give us different facets of the person of Jesus, while at the same time showing us different ways in which we might reflect the person of Jesus. We might find ourselves strongly drawn to one of the beatitudes rather than to another. If so, that is perhaps where we should focus, because it is through that particular beatitude that we might well find our own particular path to sainthood. I have always been drawn to the beatitude, 'happy those who hunger and thirst for what is right' or 'for what God wants'. My own prayer on this feast of All Saints is to ask God to help me to want what God wants.